AUTHORITARIANISM AND PROPAGANDA

The Puppet Master Tools

AUTHORITARIANISM AND PROPAGANDA

The Puppet Master Tools

J. Marcelo Baqueroalvarez

WARNING: *Read this book only if you <u>truly</u> have an open mind, if not... you are still welcome to buy it and have it readily available for whenever your mind opens up. This book will be waiting for you. This book will challenge you, pull you in all directions, and augment the way you see the world today – yes, seriously.*

Are you ready?

Copyright © 2024 J. Marcelo Baqueroalvarez.

All rights reserved. No part of this book may be reproduced, stored, or transmitted by any means—whether auditory, graphic, mechanical, or electronic—without written permission of both publisher and author, except in the case of brief excerpts used in critical articles and reviews. Unauthorized reproduction of any part of this work is illegal and is punishable by law.

ISBN: 979-8-89419-410-3 (sc)
ISBN: 979-8-89419-411-0 (hc)
ISBN: 979-8-89419-412-7 (e)

Because of the dynamic nature of the Internet, any web addresses or links contained in this book may have changed since publication and may no longer be valid. The views expressed in this work are solely those of the author and do not necessarily reflect the views of the publisher, and the publisher hereby disclaims any responsibility for them.

One Galleria Blvd., Suite 1900, Metairie, LA 70001
(504) 702-6708

AUTHORITARIANISM & PROPAGANDA
| The Puppet Master Tools

Copyright © 2023 by J. Marcelo Baqueroalvarez. All Rights Reserved.
BOOK & E-BOOK PUBLISHING FINAL PRODUCT

Copyright © 2022 by J. Marcelo Baqueroalvarez. All Rights Reserved.
ORIGINAL MANUSCRIPT AND ALL OF THE BOOK'S VISUAL MEDIA

*Published via BeeZee Vision, LLC.™, Chesapeake, Virginia, USA,
in collaboration with Half Life Crisis™, Chesapeake, Virginia, USA.*

No part of this book publication might be reproduced, stored in a retrieval system, or transmitted in ~any form or by any means, electronic, mechanical, photo-copying, recording, scanning, or otherwise, except as permitted under section 107 or 108 of the 1976 United States Copyright Act, without either the prior written permission of the Publisher, or authorization through payment of the appropriate per-copy fee to the Copyright Clearance Center, on the web at www.copyright.com.

Request to the Publisher for permission should be addressed on the web to J. Marcelo Baqueroalvarez, via BeeZee Vision, LLC at www.beezeevision.com, or via Half Life Crisis at www.halflifecrisis.com.

Limit of Liability Disclaimer of Warranty: While the publisher and the author have used their best efforts in preparing this book, they make no representations or warranties with respect to the accuracy or completeness of the contents of this book and specifically disclaim any implied warranties of merchantability or fitness for a particular purpose. No warranties may be created or extended by sales representatives or written sales materials. The advice and strategy contained herein may not be suitable for your situation. You should consult with a professional when appropriate. Neither the publisher nor the author shall be liable for any loss of profit or any other commercial damages, including but not limited to special, incidental, consequential, or other damages.

For General information about Half Life Crisis™ please visit www.halflifecrisis.com and any of our official social media accounts as listed in our main website.

Paperback ISBN: 979-8-9893753-0-1
E-Book ISBN: 979-8-9893753-1-8

HLC Control Number: 22-0800015-M

For my wife Alicia and daughter Samantha.
No matter where I might be, you two are my world and what's mine is yours. That includes my life.

CONTENTS

Page 11   FOREWORD
Page 17   INTRODUCTION

Page 19   **CHAPTER 1**
                A HIDDEN WORLD ON DISPLAY |
                Hiding in Plain Sight

Page 31   **CHAPTER 2**
                WILLFUL IGNORANCE AND APATHY |
                Making it Easier on the Puppet Master

Page 37   **CHAPTER 3**
                INTRODUCTION TO AUTHORITARIANISM |
                Politics 101

Page 51   **CHAPTER 4**
                INTRODUCTION TO PROPAGANDA |
                A Sinister Art Form

Page 61   **CHAPTER 5**
                IGNORANCE IS <u>NOT</u> BLISS |
                Letting Somebody Else Take Control of Your Life

Page 73   **CHAPTER 6**
                HISTORICAL EXAMPLES |
                The Evolution of Authoritarianism and Propaganda

                75   **Benito Mussolini | Italy**
                79   **Augusto Pinochet | Chile**
                83   **Mobutu Sese Seko | Zaire**
                87   **Hugo Chávez | Venezuela**
                91   **Fidel Castro | Cuba**
                95   **Joseph Stalin | Soviet Union**

103	**Francisco Franco	Spain**
107	**Juan Perón	Argentina**
110	**Mao Zedong	China**
115	**Vladimir Lenin	Soviet Union**
119	**Adolf Hitler	Germany**
127	**Muammar Gaddafi	Libya**
132	**Saddam Hussein	Iraq**
137	**Idi Amin Dada	Uganda**

Page 143 **CHAPTER 7**
CRITICAL THINKING |
The Real Freedom

Page 159 **CHAPTER 8**
PAIN AND SUFFERING |
WARNING Explicit Content

Page 175 **CHAPTER 9**
TRUE VICTORY |
The Adversary is Only as Powerful as his Followers

Page 193 ACKNOWLEDGEMENT
Page 195 EPILOGUE
Page 199 ABOUT THE BOOK
Page 201 ABOUT THE AUTHOR
Page 203 ABOUT HALF LIFE CRISIS™
Page 205 ABOUT BeeZee VISION, LLC™
Page 207 PUBLISHING ADMIN AND RIGHTS
Page 209 COVER DESIGN RIGHTS & CONCEPT

FOREWORD

I have been wanting to write this book for a while now. The world is not a happy place as I type these words. Unlike other books I have written before, this one will be very blunt and to the point on the current issues affecting our world. Despite this, I will not be "taking sides" – particularly because I understand that authoritarian regimes do not appreciate being called by name in any manner, they might consider unflattering.

This book is intended to help you understand the art of critical thinking and show if you are indeed under the heel of an authoritarian regime. Also, you will recognize it if you are being fed propaganda by an authoritarian-wannabe. There is a big difference between those two types. However, either one is capable of inflicting exponential damage against the safety and security of their own people. And depending on their influence, maybe even expand significant damage to other countries. It does not need to be a kinetic attack, but that is why understanding authoritarianism takes a very abstract understanding of context and historical trends.

The times when a battle was fought around the world and yielded zero side effects to the world's order are over. Most people in civilized society are sheltered from the horrors and crimes that occur every day. As you read this, somebody has been forcefully removed from their home, tortured in heinous ways, and assassinated. This is happening, and most people would not understand the suffering that is being inflicted onto other people. This book will help you put in context the realities that occur around the world – and how these might be affecting *you* right now. Even if by proxy.

A lot of people think about pain, suffering, terrorism, or any other state-sanctioned crimes as something that only happened back in ancient history. Or if that somehow still occurs, it is only in small republics that are far away from the quiet and simple lives of most civilized societies. I am here to say that believing in that rosy-colored world is willful ignorance, and it is not only wrong, but it can also be extremely dangerous.

Apathy is highly exploitable by the adversary. When we are showing willful ignorance, this becomes tacit consent to the adversary to take over our very lives. That is why it can be so dangerous.

Unlike other books I have written, this will not necessarily be provocative in nature. It will however be peppered with statements of fact, and some of those statements will not be easy to read. Much like my other books, this will also be an invitation to open your mind and enact critical thinking. This book is best read when a person is truly open-minded and enacts intellectual honesty.

True critical thinking is the archnemesis of an authoritarian. This critical thinking trait is also a perilous factor in thwarting the effectiveness of propaganda. We should understand that we are all surrounded by propaganda, often concealed under the guise of something wholesome and beneficial to the common good.

So, why am I really writing this book? You've probably heard that history tends to repeat itself. Well, it is repeating itself. A lot of the generations who are now in the driver's seat are not only ignorant, but apathic to these realities. I am writing this book to spark that curiosity that will ultimately help people wake up from this subconscious nap. We are living during precarious world events. There are too many people who are unaware of the situations that are affecting them every single day. And, most importantly, that will directly affect their future, and the future of the generations to come. This is happening, and there are many individuals out there in key positions oblivious to these facts.

And when I am talking about key positions, this spans a great gamma of professions and platforms of influence. For example, politicians, worship leaders, media personalities, bloggers, teachers, world-wide military personnel, etc.

These people in influential positions can clearly sway the power of an authoritarian figure in a positive or negative manner. But in the end, it is the individual who must be open to understanding the intricacies which prevent them from making sound decisions.

We also must realize that some people are very happy with an authoritarian status quo, especially if they are high-up in the food chain, or they perceive the antithesis is worse than their current situation. An authoritarian is only as strong as his or her followers, and we have seen a lot of that support throughout history. But you do not need to delve too far back in the past to see prominent examples of these toxic events.

As we continue to explore historical trends, you will be able to identify the realities that might be closer to your home. This might be happening right now, even as you just finished giving your undivided attention to that pretty talking head on the television who was *agreeing* with your world view. This occurs around the world more often than most people think. There is a parallel world of media and information that poses as the words of "truth," but the math does not add up. We will explore that in detail in the chapters that follow.

However, I just want to be crystal clear with you. You will realize that the chapters ahead will need a high level of abstract reading comprehension. I am going to teach you to see the world in an abstract manner. This is where the adversarial forces thrive, hidden in plain sight. Tapping in what makes you feel normal and happy. That is why it is so effective. But the world is not black and white, and this book will be able to show you how these shades of gray hold a lot more of your reality than we realize.

There are several exclusive clubs of secrets, and most of us will not be invited to these events. There are groups of people who very well understand their influence and their power. But their power is not analog to their intrinsic skill, but rather the collective support of those who believe in them as quasi-deities. We will understand how the process works, and how it enters the psyche of the population.

How it becomes an integral part of their persona. And that is the key towards understanding authoritarianism.

As I said before, I will not be talking about any current regime or world leader who is heading any of those authoritarian governments by name in this book. For two reasons, first because I do not feel like getting shot in the face by somebody who is been cited and would take my words as a personal attack. Second, because there is no shortage of authoritarian leaders. These lessons I am providing do not need to apply only at the macro scale such as world-leaders. This can be as small as the same work center or even inside a family circle. Have you ever heard about the mafia? Have you heard about gangs? These are also authoritarian organizations but on a much smaller scale.

Besides, if I do mention or talk about any country's current regime by name that would very much negate the opportunity for those who live in that area to read these words. If an authoritarian figure feels threatened, they will ban the script. That is why it is especially important to think several steps ahead about what you are planning on saying and doing.

But for example, if country x, y or z is authoritarian and they ban a book encouraging people to learn about authoritarianism, then they are likely giving tacit indication that *they are* in fact authoritarian, and they do not want their people to think freely. I do not know how far my words will travel, but what I can tell you is that there are people from all over the world who at one time or the other have felt the clutches of authoritarianism.

Another thing we will not do in this book will be leaning to either the right or left side of politics. The main reason is because authoritarianism can come from either side of the political extremes and any shade of gray in between. This happens to be one of the most contentious ways for people to either open or shut down to a new idea, even before the first word is articulated.

So, it does not matter if you lean to the left or to the right. I will be able to speak to either side and to the center. Facts do not care if you lean to either side. The facts are what they are. And that is what we will focus on. Does that mean that you might change your political stance? Maybe. Again, being to the left or right of the spectrum is not intrinsically a bad thing. There are solid governments which lean to either side, and the same is true for the opposite. A lot of authoritarians throughout history were far left or far right, respectively.

And guess what? Changing a regime from one extreme to the other could very well be as damaging to those stuck in the middle. This has happened throughout history, and by history we are also including the history that is being forged right now.

Please read my words in an objective manner. I am not advocating for an "utopia" where my views are the only true path for the future of humanity. What I am trying to do is help you gain critical thinking and teach you to fill those knowledge gaps with facts, so you can make more educated decisions as we move about this world. And most importantly, our decisions will help our next generations to be better prepared and smarter than we ever were.

As I embark on this new book, I am on board the world-famous USS COLE DDG 67. The ship is finally returning home after a nine-plus months historical deployment. We operated in the Sixth and Fifth Fleets areas of operations. There was no shortage of stories around the world that happened to touch on the topics covered in this book during that time.

Also, I prepared the template and organized the chapters for this book in the ship's "mess decks." For those unfamiliar with U.S. Navy jargon, this is essentially the main dining area for the ship's crew. This also happens to be the epicenter of the terrorist attack against this very ship in October 2000. It is a very humbling experience to be able to articulate these matters which affect the entire world while navigating on a ship that was front and center in American

History. Most of the Sailors onboard were probably infants and some were not even born when this attack occurred. Yet these Sailors are now crew members onboard this historical vessel, and they are part of the newer pages of American History onboard the very same ship.

My job onboard is analysis. I read a lot and figure out stuff... that is what I do. And being onboard for the better part of 2022 and a big chunk of 2021 – I've hyper focused on understanding the psyche of world events. A lot of what you will read will be interpretations of current events and how these events are linked to our past. Also, we will juxtapose the generational differences between what was considered the "past" and what is a continuation of an "elongated present." You will understand what I mean by that as you read through the chapters.

Nothing is as simple as it seems. There are always intricacies even in the implied simplicity. World history is written by the victors, but that does not mean that there was not a story buried among the defeated. The truth is somewhere in the middle. Where are the biases? Where are the half-truths? Where is the evidence? That can be easily controlled by either side. That is what we will explore in these pages.

Be ready to open your mind. Closed minds are fertile ground for puppet masters who will enslave you in a golden cage. Welcome to the first day of your life.

INTRODUCTION

Hello, and thank you so much for reading my book! Whatever the reason which brings you to read these words today, I am grateful because we will be discussing a lot of things that are truly relevant to our *very* survival.

Does that sound hyperbolic? It *sounds* hyperbolic, yes... but it is not. There is an entire world of puppet masters that are lurking around and holding your life and future hostage. However, much like a free-range chicken, people do not really know that they are just being given enough room to have some sort of happy existence before they become somebody's dinner. And no, you do not need to go out there and find a tinfoil hat to read this stuff.

Throughout the years propaganda has been part of our lives. Some of that is so ingrained in our own lives that we happily accept these talking points and buzz words as facts. But they are not facts, they are strategically designed to influence the very minds of everyday people. The goal is having their thoughts translate into actions in support of an authoritarian figure. That is the end game, moving rhetoric into action.

There are many intricate techniques used for propaganda, which is the favorite tool of authoritarian figures. It can even be as simple as a meme or a sound bite. For example, did you know that music has been used to give direction for the strategic mobilization of people? Well, now you know. Maybe you have never heard those songs, but they do exist, and they were jam- packed with lyrics, musical phrases and instrumentation that would create a visceral response to those listeners. Also, this technique was remarkably effective to make them remember talking points and instructions. Some of those messages were not subliminal at all. But subliminal messages are in fact a thing and have been also used throughout history both at the macro and micro levels.

This book is also full of symbolism, because I want to use that as a teaching tool. For example, there is an important reason why there are nine chapters. Nine is a divisible number, and mathematically all numbers lead to nine. So, all the lessons we are going to talk about in each chapter lead to that ultimate message. For that reason, I recommend you read this book in sequential order.

If you want to re-read a chapter at random, that is fine. But it is best if first you read the entire book in order. Otherwise, you are going to miss the proverbial train and it might turn into gibberish. Or at the very least valuable context will be missed in order to fully understand the subsequent chapter.

Also, I do not want this book to be too long. My last two book manuscripts were 300+ and 400+ pages, respectively. I have no idea how long this book will end up being. And the reason is that my intent is to give you the entire context in the shortest amount of time possible. Why? Because large swaths of the world are overdue in enacting critical thinking, that is why. Not everybody is able to see the world for what it really is. Some of us can. Information is curtailed in certain corners. Some for good, some for nefarious reasons. That is why espionage itself is such an old profession. Espionage does occur today. And part of those espionage findings helps authoritarians refine their propaganda tools. It sounds almost like a movie plot – movies are sometimes inspired by true events.

There are events right now which are peppered with propaganda. Turn on the TV, look at the internet, open a search engine. Chances are that a lot of the content you read is either an advertisement, or it has some sort of message that is designed to influence your decision making, or to exploit a bias. Granted that some of those are designed to sell you something, but the same techniques can be utilized by the propagandists to deprive you of something much more important than money, your actions and undivided attention.

CHAPTER 1

A HIDDEN WORLD ON DISPLAY |
Hiding in Plain Sight

__The best way to hide is in plain sight.__ Yes, it is happening right now. Your cell phone, your smart device, your TV, your social media – virtually everything that we take for granted today is "paying attention" and recording your every move. For example, did you know that the information on your phone is being collected by a bunch of entities? They are! Some try to sell you stuff, some others do it because they <u>really</u> want to get to know you better – and I do not mean it necessarily in an amicable way. This is why this method of concealment is so effective. What makes our lives feel normal is what also makes us vulnerable to exploitation. Does that mean that you must go out of the bounds of society and live in the wild? No, it does not. What it means is that we must learn to pay attention to our surroundings so we can enact objectivity and critical thinking.

It sounds terrible but we are all for sale – the problem is that most of us do not realize that we have already been bought and sold. Yeah, I know a hell of a way to start Chapter #1, huh? Did that opening line get your attention? Good! Because it is true. And being bought and sold happens every single day. For example, if you are using a "free" app in social media it is because YOU are the actual product. Your personal identity and private information are being bought and sold all the time. How and why do you think it is that you get all that junk mail and spam phone calls?

How does it work? Simple while paradoxically complex. Freedom is a relative term. It can be defined by having certain rights and privileges depending on the society you live in. For example, the United States of America has a bill of rights. Not every country has the same set of rights, and some have no rights at all. As you can deduce, *freedom* is very relative.

In the Unites States of America you have "Free Speech" as one of your *unmovable* rights. Can you just say whatever the hell you want? No, you cannot. There are limits to what you can or cannot say based on how this might infringe on the <u>rights of others,</u> or if it would affect public safety, or misconstrued in a negative manner that could cause or inflict actual damage onto others.

For example, you cannot just yell "fire" in a crowded movie theater if there is not an actual fire burning. Why? Because that would create panic, and this panic could result in people getting trampled down as they are trying to save their lives when they exit this place. Likewise, you cannot just speak in a derogatory or accusatory manner about somebody for alleged misconduct if you do not have proof to corroborate your claim. Otherwise, you might get hammered for slander or defamation – depending on the degree of your allegation. Defamation might be hard to prove in court, but it could happen – and the legal fees tend to be expensive either way. Bottom line, there are consequences for our actions.

But despite the consequences, there are always shades of gray. A shrewd person can read between the lines and collect a lot of information that they could use to their advantage. That does not mean that those collecting this information against a specific targeted person will be expecting instant gratification. On the contrary, it is best to "plant a seed" and harvest once this targeted soul has lowered their guard. It happens all the time. It is a mind game, and a very multidimensional game at that.

That is another reason why hiding in plain sight is so effective. We take for granted a lot of what is going on in front of our eyes. Especially if what it is on display seems mundane or "not <u>obviously</u> out of place." This is important, because the human mind has limitations on how much we perceive everything in our own environment.

It is almost like a riddle or a puzzle – one that you did not even know you were playing as an integral contributing <u>fragment</u>. In other words, the game being played upon you does not even register as such because you are not a player, you are only a token piece, much like chip or a pawn. Does it sound messed-up? It is and get used to it because this book is only getting started. At the end of this you will be hyper aware of the reality around you that we generally take for granted.

So, you might be wondering, how does this happen? As I mentioned before, our minds do not process everything that goes through our senses. In essence, our minds make "logical shortcuts" to distinguish patterns, and then our brains fill in the gaps. It is in these gaps that a skilled puppet master can infiltrate all kinds of thoughts and actions without you even realizing it. It can be so subtle that it becomes part of your own identity, and these can even hype your convictions towards this alternated version of your reality. Much like an illusionist can use tricks and misdirection to cheat your perception – similar but to a much more complex scale and execution.

Humans evolved to figure out patterns in their surroundings as a method of understanding what could affect their tenure on the planet. Much like other animals that instinctively behave in ways that seem pre-programmed without anybody "teaching them" or "demonstrating" to them what to do. For example, sea turtles. As soon as the egg hatches on the sandy beach, the baby turtles instinctively make their way to the sea. Nobody is giving them a lecture or a brief about the perils or benefits of this behavior. They are just programmed to do this from the moment they breathe the air outside their eggs. And off they go to the water.

Examples of instincts are virtually available for any animal. And of course, human beings are scientifically considered *rational* animals. This rationality sometimes *seems* to overwrite our instinctual understanding of the world. And in the blurred line between instinct and rationality is where a skilled puppet master can infiltrate all kinds of new "programming" and drive troves of people to behave in a particular manner. In fact, did you know that you can implant false memories in a person's mind if persuaded skillfully enough? It is fascinating, and it is part of our evolutionary process.

And yes, evolution is real. People do not "believe in evolution" – people either <u>understand</u> evolution or they do not. Just like you do not "believe in gravity" – you hopefully understand gravity. For those who do not if they would leap off, let us say a bridge, they will not only figure out that gravity is very real, but also that it is not the fall what injures or kills them but the sudden stop. #Science #Physics

This is another reason why propaganda is so powerful. Facts have been hijacked by unfounded opinions. And when this type of rhetoric gets enough traction, it confuses the crap out of those who lack full context and understanding for a particular subject. It does not even matter what the subject is. It could be politics, religion, save the planet, save the children, women vs. men, likes, needs, etc. The purpose of propaganda is to divide groups and galvanize those like-minded into a determinate action. Action does not need to be immediate. These seeds will be planted and harvested in due time. That method is more powerful, because it takes time to reinforce itself as an integral part of everyone targeted. That is why you will hear me say over and over throughout this book to pay attention to detail and understand context. There is a very valid reason for this redundancy.

As we age, our mind will continue to change and evolve. Notice that I did not say "as we mature." Age alone does not equal maturity – though some people would find these terms are synonymous. They are not, and propagandists will be very happy to exploit those naïve enough to think they have it all figured out. It is part of the game, getting people smart enough to do their specific bidding but dumb enough to be blind to their own reality. Those are the optimal ripe grounds for propagandists who want to manipulate others. And yes, many people are extremely naïve and willfully ignorant.

Espionage occurs in every aspect of our lives. Corporate espionage is an example. But there is one factor in espionage that is even much closer to all of us. This is called "privilege escalation." Your phone and smart devices have something known as a "backdoor." This is an access that is either programmed by the developer of an app or a device, or a vulnerability that is found by a person savvy enough to breach through the coding for said device. A backdoor would not be unlike *administrative rights* given to an information technician who manages an electronic account.

In other words, the user might get a version that is quite limited, but the administrator has a lot more access power. Some of these backdoors are legally installed in virtually every smart device you own today. But they can also be overwritten by somebody who knows how to manipulate those devices. What most of us do not realize is that we "trust" seemingly anonymous third- party entities with all our personal secrets and all our lives. And yes, these lives tend to be on full display on our smart devices.

For example, how much sensitive information do you have on your smart phone right now? Do you have any images or videos that you would not want the world to see? How many apps do you really trust? Do you know who is the developer for said apps? Do any of these apps have any access to your photos, contacts, passwords, or any other important information? How many bank account apps do you have? How many photo albums are linked to your social media accounts? How many games do you have installed on your phone?

Again, do you know who is the developer for those apps? By this I mean are they known for espionage or social engineering? Have these apps "asked for permission" to access other parts of your phone? Spoiler alert, even if it "asks" you that does not mean they are not going to access anything they want if this device has been indeed compromised. The difference is that you might not even realize that your phone is compromised.

Just rip the band aid off right now. You will thank me later. It is probably safer to assess that most devices are compromised by hackers or social engineers. These hacks can be via code lines to the device when you are visiting a site, or by clicking in a pop-up ad that seems to appear out of nowhere in a "convenient location on the screen." Also, going to certain sites that seem benign from the outside, more traditional phishing attempts such as spam email, etc. There are literally millions of ways to con a person into divulging or providing sensitive information.

And when it comes to smart devices, some of those attempts for collection are even written in the fine print nobody reads when they accept the terms of use. Why do you think many entities put those agreements in a little box you have to scroll five lines at a time when it is 100 pages long? It is by design so you will not feel compelled to read it thoroughly. That is why.

Distractions and lack of understanding of procedures are the chief way we are watched and potentially manipulated. I know, it is uncomfortable to even think about it, and frustrating to even imagine that small groups of people are essentially taking most of the world population for useful fools. That is why there will always be so many different options to keep the masses distracted. If you are distracted, then you are not paying attention. If you pay attention, you might realize where the math is not adding up. Breaking free from manipulation is a very simple concept, but it is highly complex in execution.

I will dedicate entire chapters to exploring those topics in detail. Meanwhile, I just need you to know that there is a way out of this maze. But it takes intellectual honesty and mindfulness in order to understand the abstracts of context.

If what I am telling you seems new to you, or maybe you somehow thought about it but did not give it enough credence; I just hope that you will get as much from this knowledge as possible to help the common good. Which is becoming a totally free society. There are too many lines of rhetoric out there that are hogwash and carefully designed to confuse us. At the same time, there are plenty of techniques that will seem mundane and have been normalized to divert our attention from what is really governing our lives. With this I am not saying that the entertainment industry is complicit in this, however it is instrumental to this end even if, in fact, unknowingly.

Let me give you an example. When was the last time you followed pragmatically the political platforms of diametrically opposed candidates affecting your lives? I am talking about <u>listening</u> to <u>both</u> candidates' speeches in entirety from <u>their own</u> <u>mouths</u> in order to understand their doctrines and platforms. This is different from having your news anchor or commentator of choice interpreting those words for you. Can you articulate <u>unequivocally</u> <u>both</u> candidates' platforms and doctrines? Again, I am talking about your *first account* articulation, not the interpretation from a figure head or editorial.

On the other hand, how many movies, celebrities, TV shows, short funny videos, video games, sports, memes, or other "entertainment" media consumption which are not directly relevant about how those in the ruling class are governing your life can you mention? Statistically most people will concede a lot more knowledge about the distractions mentioned in this paragraph than the facts in the previous one. Some will learn that they "have some knowledge." But again, was this firsthand knowledge or was it provided to you by your outlet of choice?

This is an important question, because most people have their "favorite" way to consume what they consider news or updates on what seems important to them. However, they potentially will either agree with one side or even vilify their opposition without even really trying to learn what the perceived contrasting groups are trying to say in the first place. This does not mean that whatever you are opposing is, in fact, correct and what you are consuming is wrong. What I am saying is that if you are taking only second or third hand accounts of what is being said – there is a probability – sometimes very high probability – that the information will be filtered before it reaches your ears. In other words, somebody has already decided on your behalf, and they are just addressing it in a way to gain your concurrence or compliance.

Propaganda outlets and "opinion" talking heads will disguise their agenda as legitimate news. This happens around the world.

In fact, some will be very professionally done to impress more mainstream audiences. But this level of flashiness is not the end-all-be-all of propaganda. There are plenty of social media pages full of memes that are in fact propaganda efforts targeted to specific audiences.

Propagandists will find the narrow focus in their target audience and push them into an echo chamber. The unsuspecting victim of this information operations campaign will often be the last one to realize this ploy – if they realize it at all. Propaganda creates useful fools. And useful fools are plenty because there is no shortage of people who think it is "too boring" to understand important issues that affect them directly. So, they will gravitate towards what seems fun and "easier to understand." This outcome too is by design, and most people will take that bait. For example, how many people you know would rather play a video game than learn about something that is affecting their very existence? I can tell you for a fact that I personally know a lot of people like that. And it is frustrating because it is willful ignorance.

I have been studying this phenomenon for several years, and I have first-hand experience in witnessing the effectiveness of this effort in the world's population. Each nation around the world and even at the local level will have their own set of information operation campaigns that plague their population in incredibly unique ways. All these campaigns have common denominators. We will delve into those details in future chapters. But for now, understand that *somebody* is driving this effort for each instance of concealed agendas. And no, you are not invited to that decision making party.

Being aware that there is a game being played and we are nothing but pawns in this even larger game, paradoxically will help you break free from this reality. Depending on how deep authoritarianism has taken a foothold in your community will dictate how hard or easy this process will be. Sadly, there are places around the world where breaking free will put your very lives and the lives of those you love at risk. Some of these restrictions can even be linked to the culture itself and have been passed through generations. Things we take for granted in one culture might be taboo and subjected to extreme punitive measures in another culture. But just because it has been a generational tradition, that does not mean that it is the right thing to do.

This type of behavior can be linked to the normalization of our environment. Tribal knowledge, tradition, "this is the way we've always done things here" type mentality. Deference or distancing for generational events can also affect this collective approach. In other words, "everybody else who we know, and respect is doing it, so it might be right," Correct? Well, no, that can very well be a logical fallacy for authority. If an idea or doctrine goes undisputed long enough then it will become part of the social fabric, and breaking those habits will be exponentially harder. Even if you know you are correct in your assessment or have factual evidence to prove that this social fabric was indeed skewed.

Let me give you a mundane example to illustrate this singularity. When I was growing up in Ecuador, there were a lot of Ecuadorians in the city I was born who literally butchered the correct use of our language by choice. They would colloquially speak with copious amounts of grammatical errors. Here is one example: In Spanish, it is incorrect to use an article before a personal noun - particularly a person's name. For example, if a man's name was "Carlos" and you were referring to him you would say something such as: *"Carlos dijo algo"* (Carlos said something). But it would be common for people in that city to say, *"el Carlos le dijo algo"* (The Carlos had said something). Which is an incorrect way to refer to somebody.

However, if you tried to correct any of your family or friends about this language fallacy, they would likely scoff and send you on your way and even try to make you feel bad for bringing it up in the first place. Because why should you be correcting something that seems to be such an insignificant detail? Despite what many would think to the contrary, this was a big deal because it gave tacit consent to start "bending other rules" in that society if it seemed socially normalized.

These small fallacies are also ripe ground to plant other "seeds" which normalize colloquial traits. As we mentioned before, some of these traits will become socially acceptable, normalized, and most people would not even bat an eye about these fallacies. These shortcomings are easily hidden in plain sight.

It is not until we ascend to a vantage point outside our own bubbles that we finally get to realize what those fallacies are, or that they even exist. That is *if* we are receptive enough to pay attention, and perhaps get over the cultural shock. For example, have you ever been in a situation where you are a proverbial "fish out of water?" In other words, either a social situation or a professional environment for which you are thoroughly unfamiliar and/or unprepared to partake.

Let us say for example, there is a man who is a placid person but somehow got hauled against his very nature to a nightclub. Let us say that this place also features very loud music, raunchy dancing, and he is surrounded by heavy drinkers. In other words, that was the last venue he would have voluntarily chosen to attend, but there he is. How well will this person be able to adapt to that environment? Well, it depends on this person's versatility. Some will probably shut down and will hate every second and could not wait to go back to their own bubble. Others might try to learn or even enjoy this otherwise unusual experience. They will realize the potential silver lining when it pertains to something they are not used to and either enjoy themselves or try to make the best of the situation. Or anything else in between.

I bring this example because I have seen these cases and I have seen both extremes and the shades of gray in between. How well people break out from their "normal surroundings" depends on the person. Some will vilify the very traits from this nightclub that I mentioned.

But I underline that if the loud music, dancing, and drinking are all consensual between adults; then that is the collective decision. Then the serene person is not by definition superior to those who are having fun in a way they have chosen to enjoy their time.

Propaganda will be able to target both extremes and all shades of gray. By "choosing the target audience," this approach is especially effective if somebody is not necessarily "versatile." Why? Because their intrinsic or acquired biases and tribalism will make them more propense to cling onto a narrow focus. That is why you will keep hearing me say repeatedly to pay diligence and understand context. There is a big complex world out there.

We all have biases and blind spots. Every one of us, and that will continue to happen until the last day of our lives. However, we can learn to control those biases and learn from our mistakes in order to minimize our vulnerability to external factors. Those factors as I keep saying are often hidden in plain sight and, as we continue with our lives, somebody is learning a lot from our behaviors and will be able to refine how they can get an upper hand on us. It is low risk to them, and high reward. And, again, if you are a target, those targeting you are not necessarily looking for immediate gratification.

If you forget literally everything I said in this chapter, please remember this: the world is not binary, it is not just black and white – it is a shade of gray and if you do not pay attention to your environment somebody will pay attention on your behalf. That does not mean *they* have *your* best interests in mind.

My challenge to you is to think about any potential way you could have been targeted. This can be either by scammers, by propagandists, by authoritarians, by religious groups, etc. Please think about this before starting on the second chapter.

CHAPTER 2

WILLFUL IGNORANCE AND APATHY |
Making it Easier on the Puppet Master

I can take ignorance; I cannot take apathy. These were the words I was telling my Commanding Officer onboard USS COLE when I first checked in as far as how I see the purview under my designation. We are all ignorant about something, we all have blind spots - every one of us. Ignorance can be fixed by imparting knowledge or context. Apathy is willful ignorance, and it is exploitable. If a person has access to and the possibility to learn something that directly or indirectly affects their lives and the lives of their loved ones but chooses to ignore it – I have a problem with that. Why? Because they are willful soft targets and subject to manipulation. This manipulation can affect many other lives around them. They are giving tacit consent for somebody else to take charge of those blind spots and use them as they best seem fit. And no, those taking control of the willful ignorant do not always tend to have the ignorant best interests at heart.

Somebody is always paying attention to what you do. Sadly, even people who feel isolated and who are "lonely" are still targeted. In fact, some of those loners can be very vulnerable to exploitation. For example, maybe a person who is lonely or has no significant other has an electronic marketplace account and buys all kinds of stuff online to fill that void of loneliness.

Another example, those alpha types who think they are the smartest people in the room. They are actually very easy targets. Even those trigger-happy who think they can shoot-fight their way out of anything. Sorry to burst that bubble. In fact, if any alphas got any reaction or are shaking their head or otherwise trying to disprove this point, I just proved that the statement alone could hit a nerve and <u>that</u> can be VERY exploitable. And they do get exploited quite often.

Alpha types tend to react passionately. Propaganda is intended to move rhetoric into action. If somebody is kind of prepped to go that way, it is easier to persuade them to follow a determinate path. They might even be very obedient to a certain cause or a "leader" who concurs with any biases that were already named by whomever is calling the shots.

But more introverted types are not safe from exploitation either. In fact, none of us are if we are not paying attention. Somebody who is attempting to manipulate you and take advantage of you does not go directly to your face and tells you: "Hey, I'm going to con or scam you for money, or to direct you do something that could get you in serious trouble of any kind." If somebody does that directly that's extortion, intimidation, etc. which are clearly illegal acts. The puppet master is not going to put themselves at that level of liability by saying something stupid like that. But he or she could very well have one or more of his minions saying something incriminating. But the puppet master will rise above the liability and have someone else carry the message and risk.

So, let us define this notorious puppet master. Who is this mystical person? Truth be told, it does not necessarily *have* to be an air breathing person. It can very well be an entire organization with many layers that either conspire together or separately. For example, a multinational ring of corporate espionage. There might be a bunch of chapters and cells that might or might not have been homogeneous to a greater apparatus. In fact, it might not be a large organization at all. You can find instances of puppet masters that can be quite small, for example cult leaders, or an authoritarian family figure. Yes, even that small.

The latter might have surprised you. There are some extremely weird families out there, and their hierarchical structure is very controlling towards the rest of their family members. Some might not even be a family member, but somebody who is sharing living quarters or dwellings. In some of these family or cohabitant structures, the "less privileged" members might or might not have any idea of the level of micro-authoritarianism they have been subjected to. It is a form of domestic abuse for sure. The difference is that there might not be an understanding for this abuse. In other words, for some families "it is what it is" – and trust me, there is no shortage of these examples out there. There might be somebody living next door to you who is suffering this fate.

Why am I starting from this micro-level puppet master? Simple, because people who might be raised in this environment are more susceptible to being controlled. I have spoken in my other books about toxic leadership and the fact that bad habits get normalized after somebody put in charge has been able to get away with doing things that would be otherwise unacceptable in a different context outside their small boundaries.

For example, have you heard about families with a strong patriarchy where the "dominant" male figure – usually the elder has unlimited authority and control over the rest of the family? These exist around the world even on this day and age, and many of those occur in segments of our own societies – not just those obscure corners people seldom think about.

The difference is that with the way the world has diversified an otherwise fringe figure could gain a lot of following and influence from like-minded people. This is very much attainable currently thanks to the globalization on social media. The world's newest and largest competition is for "attention" and if somebody is gaining a platform, this attention can galvanize intrinsic or acquired talking points. In other words, a collaboration – wittingly or unwittingly – with a puppet master who will reap the benefits.

So, if this rhetoric can be so globally influencing, why am I focusing on the family circle? Because if extreme views or lack of critical thinking has been normalized at this micro level, it creates a pre-disposition for people to follow a certain "normal." This "normal" could also be a catalyst for fear mongering, and ignoring red flags that people with a better vantage point would be able to see miles away.

As I am sitting here typing my manuscript, we are near yet another midterm election cycle in the United States of America. How many people who are in charge or have influence over groups of people do you think are following the national discourse, debates, political platforms, and doctrines, or even have any idea of what is at stake in these elections? Sadly, a very small minority.

That lack of awareness, especially from people in localized leadership positions of course translates to the subordinates. It is almost like everybody is more interested in what are the latest sport stats, or the new season of whatever show is playing. These tend to be more prominent than whatever directly will affect their very existence. And no, I am not saying that people are supposed to be pursuing a political science degree. All I am saying is that people should be giving enough attention in order to understand the intricacies of what is at stake.

Why? Because whoever is paying attention to this political discourse will call the shots. And then the apathic person who decided to rather watch a ball getting kicked down a field instead of understanding the "policies" the very candidates who will rule his/her life for the next years might, nor might not have their best interest in mind. And yes, a vote does make a difference – <u>if</u> you happen to be in a place where you can vote for whomever you decide. Not every place in the world has that option. There might be "elections," but you just "decide" to keep the incumbent or risk losing life or limb. That happens in authoritarian nations around the world.

For my American audience, understand that although voting is a voluntary privilege, it is also a gigantic responsibility. Despite this, many people decide not to vote at all, or just "guess" at the ballot, or even go down the ballot on *their* party, or vote for that person who sort of sounded like they know the candidate's name – or *that* person who seems "aligned" with their political party. But doing so without understanding the very policies and this person's record – this person who will be put in charge could become a dramatic factor in how laws and decisions will be enacted for years to come. For example, did you know that in a lot of political races there are several candidates who run unopposed for years?

And as we explore these policies on each candidate, are we following them because we like their party? Because we like them personally? Because we like their record? Because we understand and concur with their policies? Can you unequivocally answer all those questions from YOUR candidate of choice, <u>and</u> from their opponent? Did you hear it from *their own* mouth and *their official* communications or was this the interpretation given by their opposition? Think about it. It is easier to be fed lies if we have not heard or researched the actual facts firsthand. It is in our best interest to fully understand the positions of your favorite candidate <u>and</u> their opposition. Yes, you need to understand both (or in some cases more than two) sides in order to make a proper decision.

And spoiler alert, if you are one of those who could vote for a practical candidate but decide to stay home instead of voting, understand the risk. There is no shortage of people who have been fed propaganda and are ready to go to the polls and choose a candidate who will not have the best interests of their constituents in mind – especially the interests of the people from the opposite party. A lot of those problematic political figures are running for their own self-interests, but they need people to vote for them in order to get into power. And many of those toxic candidates have no shortage of following. Why do you think that is? Because they create a "need" and a "visceral response" that intensifies their followers' emotions, even if these are based on falsehoods. This is nothing new, but it works very well to this day. That is why the tactic prevails.

The common denominator is that they run technically unopposed because those who have not gained that "visceral response" would rather look away. "It is somebody else's problem," right? Not right, it is also YOUR problem. And you might very well be the cause, in part, of that problem because you did not take the opportunity to learn their policies, and make your voice heard when you had the chance. And guess what? Many countries who missed that opportunity now have no opportunity to make their voices heard at all. That is one of several reasons why apathy is exploitable.

CHAPTER 3

INTRODUCTION TO AUTHORITARIANISM |
Politics 101

At the macro level, not understanding politics will make you a willful slave to somebody else's whims. Sounds harsh? It is the reality. Political leaders come in many different stripes. Some are great, some are terrible – and by terrible, I mean authoritarian. This is not a "right or left" side of politics type argument. Either side has the ability to become authoritarian if there are no checks and balances. There is nothing an authoritarian despises more than people with pragmatical critical thinking. An authoritarian wants you smart enough to do your tasking but dumb enough not to question any inconsistencies with said tasking. And if they find themselves trapped in a corner, it is always "somebody else's fault" – because they cannot be fallible in the eyes of their – at first – adoring followers. Soon enough, this adoration will turn into fearmongering against others, and will demand unquestionable obedience. Then as the authoritarian galvanizes his or her power it will become a figure of unquestionable authority and any dissent will be met with severe repercussions. These consequences include but are not limited to intimidation, torture, or even death.
This is happening around the world to somebody as you are reading this book.

The Left and Right side of politics is a grossly oversimplified way to understand the political spectrum. For example, in the United States most people are familiar with the binary "Left – Democrats, and Right – Republican" sides. Any third party is unfortunately largely considered a fringe movement. And if you are part of any of those independent parties you will likely have to "piggyback" on to either Left or Right side of the political spectrum. What people do not realize is that between these Left and Right extremes all those shades of gray have a very wide array of political ideologies. Each one of those could be considered very "exclusive" and even eventually turn "radical" – even if at first slightly leaning Right or Left. For example, a Right-leaning person becoming a Fascist, or a Left-leaning person becoming a Communist.

Note that both extremes, though diametrically opposed, are nothing but mirror images of the same monster. Getting to either extreme can be a gradual process or exponentially accelerated based on the person's environment and the propaganda bestowed upon them.

In many other countries other than the United States of America there are dozens of political parties. In fact, the ballots encompass a gigantic choice of political doctrines. In other words, you might see a person who leans on what the USA considers "Right-wing views," but it is peppered with a lot of "Left leaning policies." And that is another reason why I am saying that the Left-Right points of view are flawed. This flaw creates this "lack of actual choice" – where people are forced to select a candidate that hopefully aligns mostly with their world view – but then possibly the voter does not agree with a lot of their platform. However, because the "other" candidate is from a <u>different</u> party, the voter will tend to choose party over actual policy.

And the sad truth is that most people who go out and vote today do so by party lines; but not because of an intimate understanding or even alignment to actual policy. At least not a pragmatic understanding of what they are "actually" voting for. People tend to gravitate towards the outlets they find "familiar." Some even take at face value that pretty person on the screen who "interprets" what the other side of the political aisle stands for. Even if that interpretation is untrue. And spoiler alert, it is often untrue, or at least spin. That is why critical thinking is important when learning about politics.

But politics is so boring! Right? Why do you think that is? Well, if you have not realized it yet, it is boring by design. Who wants to hear a boring debate about dry-policies - even if they are about something constructive? Most people will choose to just watch a ball game, or watch the last season of whatever TV show they fancy nowadays, right? The more in the dark people are about policy, the easier it is for somebody else to just give them the "cliff" notes from whatever candidate they want them to hear. It is a marketing game.

For example, when was the last time you watched a local elections debate? I am talking about the actual and <u>entire</u> debate – not just the highlights and commentary from your favorite news outlet. There is a HUGE difference between those two options. But also, there is more *science* behind the debate. Yes, politicians might lie on the debate and less informed viewers might take those falsehoods at face value because they like the guy or gal who is spewing these lies.

And that overt lie is also by design. Let us say for example in a presidential debate there are 6,000,000 viewers watching a live broadcast and a candidate says a falsehood. How many of those viewers will fact-check that lie? There is a reason why a lot of TV debates do not do an on-air fact check. The fact check might come perhaps a day, or even a few days later. The correction might also be heard only by a much smaller audience.

So, for the sake of argument, let us say that from those 6,000,000 viewers only 2,000,000 saw and acknowledged the fact-checking which indeed demonstrated the falsehood. What happens to those other 4,000,000 viewers? Some of those viewers are perhaps so enamored with "their" candidate that they might prefer not fact-checking at all. In fact, some of those viewers might even demonize anybody who dares fact-check their dear leader while calling the people who prefer the other guy or gal a derogatory epithet – or giving them a label akin to be a "sheep" or something along those lines. Some other viewers might not even care enough to see whether the facts were true or not. That is dangerous because willful ignorance and apathy is exploitable.

Paradoxically, getting fact-checked and proven wrong can <u>and</u> has been seen to get the followers of a "dear leader" to double down on the falsehood. Opinions and mistaken claims are often taken as empirical facts – depending on whose mouth those false pieces of information take genesis. The most despicable thing is that authoritarians will try to latch on otherwise actual benevolent virtues and bastardize those for their own political gain. It does not matter what it is they "advocate" for. Save the planet, save the children, religious freedom, global warming, flat earth, religious prosecution etc. No, it does not matter what it is at all, or how crazy or ridiculous it might seem. If there is a bias, then there is a way to exploit those emotions. Emotions will turn into action if the visceral response becomes significant enough to their followers.

As with anything, the more they get exposed to something the more it will become part of the person's normal identity. For example, people who are raised in very religious centric families might tend to have a misunderstanding towards other people's religions, or lack thereof. For example, how many highly devoted religious people erroneously think that atheists are devil worshipers or that atheists hate their (religious person's) deity? By the way, that is a logical fallacy. Atheists do not believe in any gods; therefore, they do not believe in any god's archnemesis either. And not believing does not equal hate. It is akin to telling them that they hate the tooth fairy. They do not, they just do not likely believe in the tooth fairy either. And they likely know that the tooth fairy is, in fact, parents putting a couple of bucks under the child's pillow if a child loses a tooth.

Why am I bringing up religion? Because religion and politics are deeply intertwined. Not just in the USA, but around the world. Religion or lack thereof are immensely powerful catalysts to mobilize people taking rhetoric into action. It really depends on how deeply your devotion lies towards a particular worldview. Some people are born in places where there is no choice but to follow whatever deity was geographically assigned to that area. And before you jump at my throat about that statement, look at any map of the world and see what the predominant religion for each area is. You will realize the obvious – different areas of the world tend to conglomerate specific religious leanings. With that said, believe whatever makes you a good person who respects everybody's diversity. Yes, diversity is a good thing. Authoritarians will try to convince you that the opposite is true.

This is one of the reasons why politics and religion tend to become taboo topics in several arenas. For example, in many western professional organization politics and religion views are to be kept internalized so as to not create what could be considered a "catalyst for dissent" among the people in those groups. Why? Because politics and religion tend to be very emotionally charged topics. There are people who will either end friendships, shun family members, or even disavow loved ones because of dissenting opinions on these topics. Hence the reason why these discussions tend to be generally taboo.

However, I would argue that understanding politics and religion in a pragmatic and mature manner is a positive thing. I would even dare to say a virtue. Why? Because it expands critical thinking, and it even helps you to galvanize the understanding of your own religious and political views in an objective manner.

Unfortunately, there is this fear that getting religion and politics scrutinized would create a false dichotomy or even lead to mayhem. But the opposite is true, if these topics are approached with an open mind and intellectual honesty. That is the problem though, most people fail on unequivocal objectivity and pragmatism when speaking about their own religion leanings or political affiliation. And of course, certain religious or political leaders will feel threatened if a person gains more factual knowledge about dissenting views. It is not convenient for them, because it could result in attrition.

If you are one of those people who are very devoted to your religion or your political party, I invite you to open your mind objectively. You will learn a lot about yourself. I would be remiss if I did not emphasize that there is a risk your world view might be affected, or even fly against whatever you thought to be true and accurate until then. Millions of people who went through that process experienced exactly that. But although it was usually a challenging experience, they gained a lot of introspection and greater understanding about their reality from this experience. That is a win!

I will not sugar coat it. Even for people who are otherwise considered very tolerant and open-minded, this level of introspection can in fact present a gigantic self-challenge. Why? We are usually more adept to be "objective" when we are assessing factors that are <u>external</u> to our own visceral and emotional responses and environment. Looking inside towards what would constitute a direct challenge to our own convictions, our environment, and even those who we unequivocally trust and admire can be a gigantic conundrum to afront. People will tend to perform very elaborate mental gymnastics to rationalize why and how their world view is the correct one. Even though it would fail to hold its own under unbiased scrutiny with the same rigor and metric as they would scrutinize dissenting views.

That does not necessarily mean that these diametrically dissenting world views are erroneous. But not being objective will open the door for logical fallacies to permeate the assessment of dissenting world views vis-à-vis our introspection.

With this context now we can go ahead to the next part of understanding the political spectrum.

Most people erroneously think the political spectrum is linear, like the example in the next page. This depiction is ideal for the puppet master because it will intrinsically create a division between dissenting opinions. Please look at the graphic in the following page, analyze it and let us discuss further.

In this graphic you can see that extreme left is depicted as *Communism*, and the extreme right as *Fascism*, and a "centrist" somewhere in the middle ground between non-extremist left and right leanings. From the onset it does look like that simplified construct is practical until you realize how the political spectrum is really laid out.

INTRODUCTION TO AUTHORITARIANISM | | 43

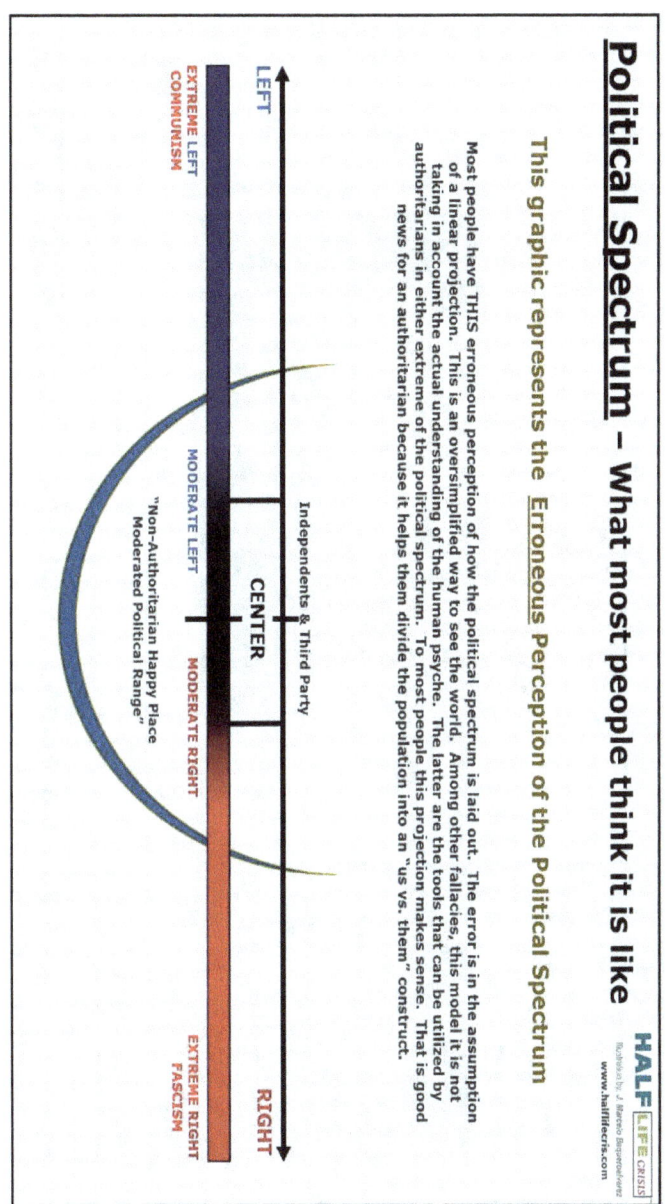

The correct spectrum is not linear but more like a horseshoe. Please, look at the graphic on the next page and take a moment to study the similarities and differences in your experience.

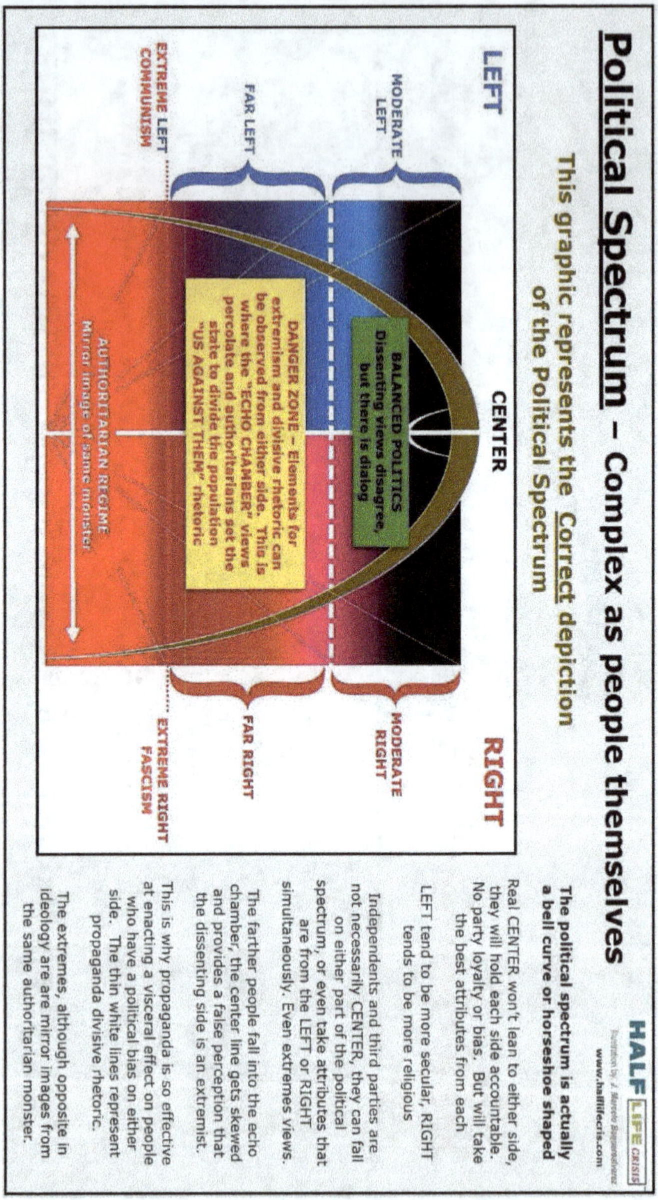

As you can see, this is a very different dynamic. For the similarities, the Extreme-Left is still Communism, while the Extreme-Right is Fascism. The further people go to either extreme of the political horseshoe the more radicalized the ideology and their followers will become. Note that authoritarianism becomes a mirror image of the same extreme view the further a person descends into radicalization. As previously mentioned, this radicalization process can be gradual or accelerated based on the person's socio-political environment.

If this socio-political environment seems to concur with a particular ideology; even if this ideology is in fact mistaken in substance or accuracy – but commonly accepted as truth by this person's circle of influence and familiarity – then their natural inclination will be to believe what seems "normalized" to them.

In other words, if everybody in their circle of friends, family, congregation, and other people that these individuals admire, respect, or otherwise emulate this figure, then they will be most likely to believe anything that is been communicated to them by this normalized group. This inevitably will create the rest of that group to repeat certain taking points and ideas that concur with each other's preconceptions. That is normal, but it can be dangerous when the information and talking points are not actually based on fact. That is what is known as an echo chamber. People with similar world views recycling their own uncontested talking points – without really understanding what the perceived dissenting point of view is all about.

That would beg the question, how do people differentiate, or can they even realize if they are being placed in an echo chamber? For some people it will be very easy to realize if the narrative is false, and for others it will be extremely difficult or even impossible. The difference from each group is intellectual honesty and the ability to listen, analyze and understand what a potential dissenting opinion is <u>actually</u> about.

Normally this group of people who can understand those intricacies are at the very top of this political horseshoe. These are the *actual* centrists. This is a person or ideology that does not necessarily concur nor dissents with all the "traditional" Left or Right political leanings. Instead, they will tend to pick any or all attributes they find more closely aligned with their own perception of what is adequate or not. In other words, there is no blind loyalty towards a particular political party or politician, or individual in power.

Although there are exceptions, centrists will normally be better informed on both and/or either side of their political spectrum. However, when a person is being pushed into an echo chamber, the propagandist will make them feel like they are the smartest person in the room. Almost as though they are reading their mind, and everything else in their potential narrow scope of view is spot on. This is especially effective if a complex narrative is oversimplified. Context and actual critical thinking will be lost. We will speak more in-depth about this topic in a different chapter later on in this book. For now, I just want you to understand that any political leaning on either side of the aisles might come with more baggage than what meets the eye. There is a reason for that also. And shrewd political campaigns can capitalize on those shades of gray. However, they will look very much black and white to those who are unfamiliar with the intricacies of this process.

Between the centrist and the Left and Right leanings you will find the entire gamma of different political views. Some of these will be more homogeneous, some will be more dissenting. Especially if the ideologies are mirror images from each other. Depending on the projection there is in fact a gigantic number of political leanings. That is why I mentioned earlier that the binary system is flawed. There is a lot more complexity in the political spectrum than just the mistaken one-dimensional Left and Right political leanings perception by the general public.

However, even in this construct there are going to be ebbs and flows on political leanings. Why? Because people are complex, and as such they either incite potential constituents into a particular leaning or start learning more about other political doctrines. Their political views will also adjust accordingly. Some of these changes will be good. In other words, a person is getting better informed, and understands the gamut of political intricacies on a platform. Thus, it helps them reach better educated decisions when it comes to voting and political involvement. Or, on the other side of the spectrum it can be used for evil, and they could get potential constituents radicalized under the direct or indirect tutelage of a puppet master. And the latter – as previously mentioned – could even happen unnoticed based on the potential constituent's environment and their individual or collective cultural upbringing.

What do I mean by environment and cultural upbringing? We are all products of our experiences and our upbringing. Some of us will be able to break free from an otherwise stagnate environment which advocates for blind obedience and unquestionable faith towards whomever was put in charge. Being this authority symbolizes a person or even a deity.

Culturally speaking, each culture will instill a sense of belonging and perhaps it is better described as a cohesive identity between its members. And I said perhaps, because some cultures already assign roles to their people from birth. Some of which will be relegated to the back of the proverbial bus, and some will be born into a higher hierarchical status. This phenomenon also occurs today and has occurred since the beginning of civilization. Authoritarians prefer this construction because this provides a unilateral power structure where they stay on top of the food chain. Not surprisingly, this is not in the best interest for that entire society, only to those on the top echelons in that cultural structure.

Also, we must remember that great swats of people are more interested in hearing what they "want to hear," regardless of if what they are hearing is the truth or a falsehood. These falsehoods may very well be the product of conspiracy theories. And people who have been pre-disposed to believe these unsubstantiated and false claims tend to also become very stubborn if presented with empirical facts that contradict their misperceptions.

This blind-follower stubbornness tends to cling to skewed realities and constitutes the main problematic factor that people who fight against authoritarians need to contend with. The extremist who believes these conspiracy theories will also tend to get lost in the irony for their own misunderstanding. Whilst claiming in a pedantic manner their mistaken assertion as unequivocal certainty. This is in-fact a cult-like behavior people will pursue because it gives them a sense of identity. However, this is not a *real* identity, they are being lied to. That is why when speaking politics and religions, emotions must be tempered. Otherwise, the belief of dissention will push them further into their false reality.

Some might ask, why am I talking so much about this misinformation? Because in order to truly understand politics, you must understand who the actual constituents are. There is an intrinsic need to understand what makes this political base galvanize their support behind you, or the person, or people who will be categorized as the leadership for that group. Leaders, and people put in charge of any stripes – to include authoritarian figures are only as powerful as the people who will endorse their rhetoric, behavior, and doctrines.

What political affiliation will you subscribe to? That is up to you. There is nothing intrinsically malign about being to the right or the left of the political spectrum ideology. People will disagree on certain points of view and doctrines. That is normal. It is true that some people will find their point of view more adequate than their opposition. However, that consensual and bipartisan discussion is not what we are talking about in this book. We are talking when the dissent goes awry and the objectivity gets lost in the mix, pushing this political leaning to extreme. All extremes are bad. Remember that.

Some political views seem to be working fine if everybody is afforded a dignified existence, and where their efforts allow them to make a living. In other words, working for a living and not living for working. In an authoritarian regime people do not own their time, their labor, nor the fruits of those factors. That is why it is imperative to understand seemingly dissenting political views and recognize the underlying narratives. That will enhance this important level of critical thinking.

Politics is supposed to be the science that helps govern a group of people. There are many types of government, and although no government is 100% perfect, there are many examples of good leadership figures throughout history. But just as there are good examples, there is no shortage of terrible regimes who have caused mayhem, destruction, genocide and so many other atrocities against their own regime and humanity at large.

In many instances before authoritarians were "elected" into power, the writing was on the wall. There were indicators of people trying to warn about the looming danger. Many of those warnings fell on deaf ears and were dismissed, and subsequently the malign consequences forewarned were spot on.

Some other authoritarians reached power by force, or via a coup. There is a non-zero chance that as soon this figure attained power all people with dissenting points of view were either forced to play ball and color up or be killed. These crimes against humanity do happen, and we will talk more about that in a later chapter.

The reason I am speaking about it here is because if you are one of those lucky individuals who lives in a society where you can vote, yet you choose not to vote – you are wrong. You just have no idea what you are taking for granted by dismissing that right. So many before you risked all, and many more gave their lives for you to have this privileged opportunity afforded only to so few – if compared to the rest of the world at large.

Please understand that the world is and has been host to many authoritarian regimes. But some of those regimes were not a closed society for the entirety of their existence. There are places where a figure got into power at some point in its history, and from there on the population was forever stuck with this person – or the same frame of authoritarian government.

In other words, taking for granted what you consider today as freedom and liberty of expression can very well come to an end, based on who has been afforded the opportunity to gain unilateral power. And yes, this power-grab can be gradual. It will start slowly, and once it has been galvanized enough, it will wrap its tentacles exponentially fast. That is why proper education, critical thinking, and intellectual honesty are so important.

CHAPTER 4

INTRODUCTION TO PROPAGANDA |
A Sinister Art Form

Propaganda is alive and well today as it has been from the beginning of societal times. *Propaganda is a distorted reality which is packaged in a way that will be easily consumed by a particular group of people. The end state is turning rhetoric into action. The type of action will depend on the goals and tactics delineated by the puppet master with said propagandistic efforts. Some of these actions will seem passive, such as the population just giving the "dear leader" their undivided attention when asked. Or it might be an active manifestation such as unswerving obedience. This latter one may escalate to donations of time, money, and effort. And of course, this obedience could even lead towards a call for arms intended to defend the "dear leader" from his or her perceived enemies. Propaganda will portray these obedient followers as righteous people. This will enable the puppet master to sink this group into what is known as an echo chamber. This is when dissenting opinions are demonized and only the "official words" from the "dear leader" are to be heard and followed to the letter – because according to the leader everybody else has a "nefarious agenda." This is happening right now around the world, and not even too far away.*

Stochastic Terrorism is the ultimate sign of obedience that victims of propaganda will enact against the "dear leader's" perceived foes. The process is going to take time, and like any other successful production it starts with finding a receptive target audience. Whenever a commercial, a movie, a TV series, or any product is created the first question a savvy producer will ask is: Who is going to buy this product? In this case the product is a particular rhetoric or world view.

This is also true in the preliminary planning stages for a coup. Yes, even if the authoritarian figure takes power by force, it will take some calculation and planning. There have been many unsuccessful coups throughout history, and they failed when they overestimated their chances for success. Why? Because this authoritarian wannabe will need people and minions to support this campaign. An authoritarian without followers is just a crazy eccentric individual screaming platitudes into a void.

But if these platitudes are being received by a receptive audience, this can change their position from the ramblings of a madman or madwoman into the perceived *"wisdom of a dear leader."* Sometimes slowly, sometimes exponentially fast. It depends on the predisposition of this person's potential followers. Whomever is providing support on the earliest stages will likely become one of the authoritarian's inner-circle "trustees." But that does not mean this authoritarian figure might not dispose of these loyal followers once their usefulness has expired.

When it comes to authoritarianism, propaganda is the favorite tool because it can spread like wildfire. If the authoritarian can find fertile ground for propaganda in the minds and emotions of his or her followers, then it becomes as easy as convincing a small group of useful fools to run with a narrative and see it how quickly it becomes part of the societal fabric being targeted. And as I mentioned before, this authoritarianism can be at the macro level such as world leaders or micro level as small as a local government or even a family.

For example, many cults will have their own propaganda. Their "official literature" will be the only "real truth" about what they are all about. Their cause, their doctrine, among other things that make them "unique" from the rest. But only a very small group on the top of that cult's food chain will know that the no-kidding "real truth" is only a façade to galvanize and sustain the support from their obedient followers.

Authoritarianism thrives in this projection and that can very well include cults of personality. The authoritarian will be so "grand" and "benevolent" – although stern and implacable against definitive enemies of their cause – which can include any former obedient followers who got out from the circle of trust. Again, it does not matter what the cause is, whatever is it they are "defending." There *will* be an archnemesis who is very strong – but also weak – and can only be defeated by *this* group alone.

For example, let us say the cult is of a religious variety. This one type of religion-lite who is against other groups who do not take them seriously. The next logical step will be propaganda. The cult leadership will either demonize or skew the dissenting doctrines to spur support against a perceived foe. Here is a contemporary example: There are violent religious extremists who happen to be Shia Muslims who are attacking Sunni Muslin nations every other day (at the time this manuscript is being written). But there are also violent extremists who happen to be Sunni Muslims who also conduct crimes against humanity based on *their* misinterpretations from *their* religious doctrines. So, yes, it can be two opposing forces blinded by propaganda against one another – and still both sides of that equation are being erroneous. Why? Because people are more complex than a binary right or wrong. That is one reason why propaganda can be so powerful and enticing for so many.

In either case if there is a "dear leader" or ultimate top figure in the group who oversees a cadre of "loyal top tier followers." It is the top person who is essentially calling the shots. But most of the *actual* violent acts tend to be delegated to the lower tier of followers. In fact, some obedient followers will be even convinced to give up their very lives for the dear-leader's cause on suicidal missions.

And if you think that only happens in radical examples of the Muslim world as described two paragraphs ago, think again. There are also plenty of contemporary and historical acts of radicalized Christian groups who committed horrendous crimes against humanity. A common historical example is the inquisition. There are thousands of other examples spanning every imaginable religion too. I am not going to delve much further into the religious differences in this book. I wrote an even longer book than this very book you are reading right now, where I speak about world religions and atheism.

This point for <u>this</u> book is that religion is <u>also</u> an extraordinarily strong motivator and, in the past (and present), became tacit justification to commit acts that would not only be considered illegal, but even genocidal. Again, it is the <u>followers</u> who ultimately perpetrate the crimes mandated by a top figure.

The saddest part is that these people who end up committing crimes or turn into nefarious actors might have been bamboozled into committing these actions in the first place. But make no mistake, we all have the ability to do extreme things if the environment and the circumstances place us in a precarious situation. Even if this precarious perception is a falsehood. And this versatility of action can be used for good or for evil. For example, in case of emergency a person who is otherwise a very low-key introvert might get out of their comfort zone and take charge of the emergent situation and render help when or if everybody else freezes.

But the opposite is also possible. Some people can be prepared to respond to a manufactured crisis. In other words, there is not an actual emergency – but the rhetoric creates a sense of division. Then suddenly, this non-issue becomes a political football. It does not matter what the issue is. That is incidental at best – the goal is to create division and to separate and rank the levels of loyalty towards the "dear leader." Ultimately the narrative will be about the "issues" at hand – though some issues will have some intrinsic merit, they are also essentially just vehicles to run the rhetoric. And remember, the end state is to turn rhetoric into action.

So yes, there is an underlying reason why I am adding some strategic redundancy in this book. And I realize that some of the concepts might seem abstract to a casual reader. Maybe you will also feel that way as you are reading these sentences. Some might even feel these concepts are difficult to understand. It is intended to be this way. As you read my pages, I do not just want to give you a "watered down version" about authoritarianism. My intent is to train your mind to see these often-hidden abstract dynamics. That is where the authoritarian thrives. The propagandists want to show you an oversimplified "concrete world," so the important details can hide behind the more obscured intricacies people assume or take for granted. Especially those details who might seem tangential or even totally unrelated to the topic at hand. That is why propaganda can reach so many people virtually unnoticed.

Much like an illusionist would use misdirection and other techniques to present a "reality" to the audience; the propagandist will present a version that is on the surface for "wide consumption" that does not really reflect the actual mechanics for their true intent. In other words, there is more to the story than what is shared with their loyal fan base.

Please do not feel bad if you have been a victim of propaganda before. Statistically speaking, everybody on the planet has been a victim of some sort of propaganda at some point in their lives. It is part of the learning process. At some point we have all had the ability to be over-trusting and get emotional about a particular topic we feel very much connected to. In fact, there are languages where "propaganda" will be used as synonymous as the word "advertising." It is designed to be that way. That is why there is an entire industry dedicated to the psychology of advertising.

As I mentioned in an earlier chapter, the more we get exposed to a projected reality, the more it gets normalized and becomes part of the status quo. In other words, it becomes the "it has always been that way" – even if nobody really remembers the origins for that "tradition" everybody in the community seems to embrace. But this can also happen when we are barraged by narratives that try to pass opinions and misinformation as empirical facts.

For example, pay close attention the next time you go to any search engine portals where several entities display news or other articles.

How many of those are legitimate news, and how many of those are actual advertising disguised as news? You might or might not be surprised to learn that some "news" outlets are in-fact just advertisement for some narrative. In other words, the *news story* is an actual ad, aside from all the other traditional ads they display.

This is dangerous, because then the real news gets obscured by information that is successfully pushing a false narrative. And to that point, you must remember that your smart devices are always analyzing y<u>our</u> behavior. These devices feed algorithms that will prompt more content that is similar to what you were just looking at. This is a marketing tool, hopefully just trying to sell you stuff. However, this same principle can be very effective when an entity is pushing propaganda.

We spoke about brand loyalty in a previous chapter. This is related to that. Once a person has accepted to give undivided attention to a person or a topic, then it is easier to bring more information to feed their perceived curiosity. Pseudoscience and other "half-truths" will be particularly important in order to sell a narrative. In other words, there will be "some truth" to whatever false claim they are making in order to be considered legitimate, and not immediately discarded as conjecture. How does this work? Well – this is the art form that makes advertising and propaganda alike effective. There are literally millions of ways to achieve this goal.

Why? Because there are several billion people in the world, and each person is unique. Propaganda will not be able to convince 100% of the population about a false narrative, but it does not have to. It just needs to convince a determinate percentage of loyal followers and let it grow from there. In fact, some of those loyal followers will be so convinced about a narrative that they will be willing to get it pushed onto others, even if that requires the use of force, coercion, or even violence.

Every authoritarian regime in history started as first a fringe movement, but eventually they took on enough people to "legitimize it" and then they continued to grow. True that some might have gotten a higher platform at the beginning. But one common trend is that a great majority of the opposition did not take them as a serious threat until it was too late. Complacency from the potential opposition is a great ally for the authoritarian. Remember, tacit consent by inaction. But then again, authoritarian propaganda will look like a welcomed rhetoric to those who do not understand the complexity for the potential consequences.

If you give a lie long enough time to grow, eventually some people will not even realize it was all make-belief. Especially if a lie endures through generations, or if the original dissenting records are erased or concealed from history. That is why authoritarian figures are generally anti-actual-critical thinking, anti-science, and would be happy to conduct book burnings or other cultural "cleansings" doctrines. These actions could evolve – and in some instances have evolved throughout history towards genocide.

And this is one of the most sinister aspects of authoritarian propaganda. Otherwise "common-every-day-people" are incited to commit acts which go against any shred of humanity and decency. How can this occur? Well, if it was not obvious enough, it is because this division and mentality of "us against them" will ultimately dehumanize their perceived adversary. For some people, this process might be very quick, and for others it might take years of brainwashing.

But the problem is that we are all vulnerable to commit acts of extreme violence if the circumstances seem dire enough. In other words, the "flight or fight response." It is this animalistic instinctual nature that can be awakened in people, even if in their own minds they think they are the nicest people in the world. For example, have you ever gotten angry? But I am not talking about regular anger, I am talking about furious rage. Maybe you were not able to act upon those impulses due to whatever boundaries that prevented you from descending into an instinct- driven-rage which could end up being a potential criminal offense. In other words, something, or somebody was able to calm the situation (even if it was yourself) and defuse the rage enough to prevent a catastrophe from occurring.

But what if you felt entitled to commit such a violent action? And what if you even got condoned and essentially sponsored to commit this aggravating act? And just for good measure, you feel justified about it as though it was some sort of vindication? Some people do not have an intrinsic-self-activated "stop" button to understand these limits when they are victims of the very environment that incites them to act violently with impunity. That is how countless crimes against humanity started. The startling part is that this formula works, and it has worked since humans started roaming the Earth.

But surely, you would think that several millennia after men started living in society became more adept to understand the sinister intricacies. Well, no. There are a lot of examples in history where instances of great violence will be followed by a relatively peaceful time. During this "peace time" a lot of complacency occurs. It is when "this cannot happen to me" way of thinking percolates. It is a logical fallacy, because evil (and not talking about a devil or demon but rather the actual malice that exists on the instinctual depths of each human being) can be channeled by a skilled charlatan.

The most despicable thing is that the propagandist who aligns with an authoritarian will inevitably cling on actual wholesome values as the catalyst to grab their potential follower's attention. There must be a conflict, there must be "bad adversary who is so powerful, but at the same time very weak. And only *this* group of people have been *destined* to end this injustice." The "chosen ones" – as they will self-proclaim – will become enticed to pay closer attention to this potential adversary. And based on this attention, they will be able to escalate their participation to align themselves with this "visionary" leader who has been put in charge.

What is the cause they are fighting against? It does not matter; this rhetoric is only incidental. It will be whatever bias that can be best exploited. This will be the followers' insecurities, their lack of understanding over *something* – they are *now* against, their apathy, their lack of intellectual honesty, their blind obedience, their strong drive, even their cynicism. These can be channeled by an authoritarian to gain support from otherwise good people. In other words, propaganda will find their weaknesses and weaponize these against *their* adversary – which is in reality the *authoritarian's* adversary. In other words, the followers have just become useful fools and errand boys and girls for the propagandist. Remember, the authoritarian is only as strong as those who choose to follow him or her.

CHAPTER 5

IGNORANCE IS <u>NOT</u> BLISS |
Letting Somebody Else Take Control of Your Life

Most people have heard that those who fail to learn from history are doomed to repeat it. And I say most people because today, despite the fact we have more knowledge about the known universe at our fingertips, we are surrounded by willfully ignorant people. Quite honestly it is baffling and paradoxical that the more information is available to us, the more people are unwilling to learn facts, and rather favor any form of entertainment, or even conspiracy theories. Meanwhile they will leave the "important stuff" for "somebody else" to think about that. "Because it is boring, or if it is too hard to understand." In the willful ignorant minds, they erroneously perceive it is probably not worth learning about the actual important facts anyway. I have said it during my time in uniform, I can take ignorance, but I cannot take apathy. Ignorance can be resolved by providing information and enacting critical thinking. But apathy is exploitable, because willful ignorance gives tacit consent to somebody else
to take control over your destiny.

I find it disheartening, we live in the most technologically advanced moments in our history thus far. Yet the world is populated by large swaths of willfully ignorant people. I cannot begin to tell you how many times I have met people who assert that ignorance is bliss. And superficially it might seem so, because learning about the complexities that govern our lives is multifaceted, can be very abstract, and it can certainly be overwhelming – dare I say even depressing. But the fact that many people decide to look away from their reality does not make this reality disappear. They are just giving tacit consent for many unsavory consequences to occur without their knowledge or understanding.

Authoritarians love it when their followers lack critical thinking and intellectual honesty. These authoritarians will be ok with "critical thinking" to a point. Essentially, the authoritarians will be ok if their followers can use flawed logic in a cynical manner. In fact, there is no shortage of people who spew all kinds of mistaken information with a high degree of confidence, even though they are extremely wrong on the factual merits. And authoritarians love using these types of followers. They are smart enough to do their bidding, but too dumb to understand they are nothing but a disposable tool in the authoritarian's sadistic ecosystem.

Make no mistake, we all have blind spots, and we all are ignorant about something. In fact, we are ignorant of so much that exists out there. But that does not mean that we should stop learning as much as we can about what surrounds us. Back in the Middle Ages doctors thought they had to bleed people to cure all kinds of diseases. Now we know that these old doctors were wrong on those doctrines. But it is because science continues to evolve, and we continue to learn from past mistakes.

But we do not have to go that far back in time. Today, most everybody has at least one smart device in their possession. Being a cell phone, a tablet, a smart TV, a smart refrigerator, a smart speaker, a smart watch, etc. We are connected to the internet in ways just a few years back were something akin to science fiction. Go back in history far enough and that technology would have been considered magic or even witchcraft.

I remember when I was a young adult in the 90's, having a cell phone was an insane luxury. The phones themselves looked like bricks, the signal was terrible, the cost per phone call was astronomical – and that was even for a local call. Calling long distance, even to a different city would set you back a small fortune. In fact, even on a land line it was a big deal to be super brief on the phone. Especially if you were calling over a long distance. Even if you were talking to a loved one whom you missed very much you had to be very brief or pay a lot for that chat. Nowadays, you can make a video call virtually for free from your cell phone. In fact, it is funny that most people use their phone for pretty much everything except making actual voice phone calls. Text ok, messages ok, video chat ok, phone calls… very rarely nowadays – at least for non-official use.

Personally, I never answer the phone if it is a number I do not recognize. And I know I am not the only one out there following the same logic. Why is that? Because I know better, a lot of times if I answer an unknown number is some kind of scam artist who is trying to pull a fast one. Yes, your number and personally identifiable information is bought and sold every day to people who will call you, hopefully just try to sell you something. Unfortunately, a lot of those calls are scammers who will be trying to separate you from your money in any way possible and available to them. This happens all the time, to somebody. As we read this, somebody else has fallen victim again.

But with all these emails, phone, and text message scams being decades old you would think that people would be wiser by now, right? Well, no. That is why old and new scams continue – because people keep falling for them. And by the way, scams and swindles are not even "technically" illegal. The way the law is written in several jurisdictions will see it as "if you are dumb enough to fall for a scam, then sad day for you. You should have paid more attention." However, fraud – which is not necessarily the same thing, though remarkably similar in execution is a felony under many jurisdictions and can put a person in jail… if you can prove it. By the way, it can take a lot of money in legal fees. Surprise!

So, as you can see, this is already an applicable example of how ignorance is not blissful. In fact, it can be painfully expensive and inconvenient. But sadly, many people would rather take that gamble and remain ignorant, often by giving their attention to any other activity – rather than understanding how the world around them really works. And that includes how directly or indirectly politics affects them.

And yes, the world will affect you even if you are not aware of how it is affecting you. The difference is that when you know or at the very least have some awareness of what is affecting you, then you can formulate a plan and perhaps break this cycle of powerlessness. Hopefully shifting the probabilities in your favor. The results might not be immediate. In fact, it could take a long time before you can see any tangible results, but at least you will be moving in the right direction.

And that is the actual crux of vulnerability. When people finally gained awareness and are trying to move in the right direction, but the results seem to be awfully slow to concrete, then these well-intentioned people might tend to get discouraged and walk away towards a familiar or "easier" direction. Authoritarians and propagandists are very much hoping the latter will be the outcome this otherwise well-intentioned person will follow. Self-defeating of a well-intentioned person makes it a lot easier for their adversary to succeed and prevail.

Another problem that could occur, and this will sound counter intuitive, pertains to small victories that can be attributed in great part to luck and chance. These cases could create a false sense of security, and even be used as the leverage of "being there done that" and touting it as success. I have seen this happen in every stratum of leadership from the micro at a home, to the strategic with peer level nations.

For example, the Cuban missile crisis. If you are unfamiliar with this, during the Cold War the Soviet Union was executing a plan to place nuclear missiles in the island of Cuba less than 100 miles from Florida. There was a lot of luck involved in this event to prevent nuclear Armageddon. This happened during the Kennedy administration. The non-destructive resolution was also in part aided by the expertise and temperance of the world leaders on how they oversaw this delicate situation. But this does not negate the fact that there were thousands of collective decisions made by either side that led to the Soviet Union's decision to place those missiles in Cuba in the first place. Today, even though the world could have ended well before many of us were even born; for many people it is either something akin to a cliff note in history, and for many others an event they had no idea existed.

And that is yet another reason why I say that ignorance is no bliss. Even back then, there were people who had no idea about the Cold War, or worse chose not to pay attention to it, nor to the effects this could have had in their very lives. Regardless of their cognizance they all would have still gotten vaporized in a radioactive cloud. Yes, regardless of whether they were paying attention or not. But because some people were indeed paying attention, this world-ending problem was then mitigated by following the procedures available to them at the time.

It is easy to look away, and the truth is that it is hard to figure out what exactly are the topics that we should be focusing upon. Entertainment is not necessarily a willful deceitful factor in this equation of diverting our attention from what really matters. But it can indeed be an exploitable factor if somebody has an agenda and wants to keep us looking away from important issues. And the fact is that this approach works very well because the less attention we pay to our surroundings and live inside these lenses of entertainment, the less we will be able to understand patterns that might affect us negatively.

And to make sense of this, let me give you an example. Let us say there is a ball game and a debate about several opposing political candidates being broadcasted at the same time. The outcome of this election could affect the lives of millions of people for years to come. Especially because there are a few very extreme viewpoints debating on this stage. Which one of these two events should we pay closer attention to? The ball game or the debate?

Rhetorical question, plenty of people will choose the game. And why not, right? It is fun, they see their favorite players, enjoy a time munching on snacks and chugging beverages with their likeminded folk. There is no other stress than if their team loses (because *that* would be traumatic to some sport fans). Besides, who wants to use their free time to do something boring such as watching a debate, right? It is party time to watch the game at home. Everything else can wait. These professional league millionaire ball players are getting all the attention today.

And no, I am not against sports. What I am trying to illustrate is the timing of these two distinctive events – and their potential impact. Which event should take priority? Of course, the entire sports industry would say the game, of course. And guess who else wants that? The more radicalized candidates, because they can now spew whatever they want and just add their talking points to the debate lines. They know that the controversial lines will make headlines, and that is possibly the only thing that most of the otherwise distracted people will be paying attention to. And perhaps vote on the zingers, rather than the actual policy. But if a person watches the entire debate pragmatically, then hopefully they will be able to understand the nuisances and the entire context.

And context, that is what the propagandists and authoritarians want to muddy out. When a person does not understand the context then the pattern, and the details get buried. But then these loose talking points tend to be given a superficial legitimacy as facts when they are in fact conjecture at best. However, to the casual observer these fallacious talking points will be perceived as empirical truths. And yes, it is designed to be that way. That is intended to supply a little bit of truth or plausibility to an otherwise totally erroneous statement. And then superficial fact-checking will seem as though the talking point was a statement of fact, even if the factual part is only a small percentage overall. That is why context matters.

In a separate book I wrote titled:

LEADERSHIP | Understanding the Human Factor

I have covered the Dunning Kruger Effect. I will not go as deep into this chapter as I did in that book, but it is important to understand its relevance on this topic. In essence the Dunning Kruger Effect is whenever you find a person who thinks they have a mastery level of understanding on a particular topic, just because they have a bit of correlation on a cause.

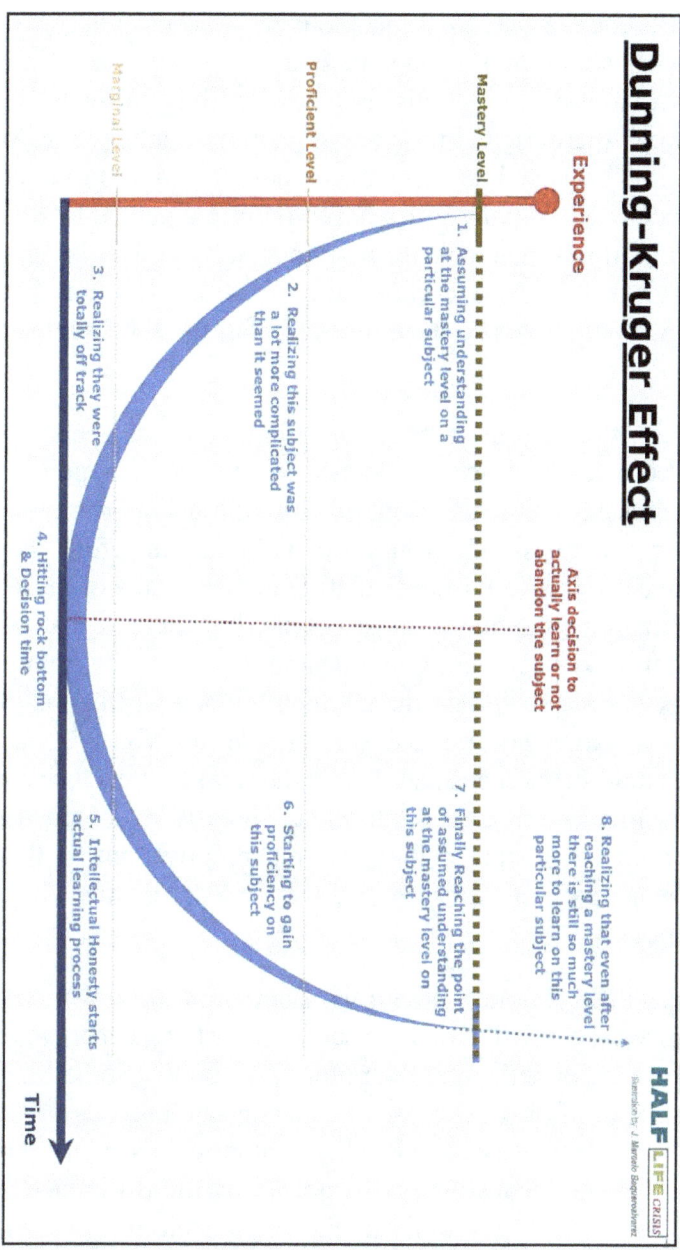

It does not matter what topic this may be, it can happen to anybody, we all have blind spots.

The difference is that some people clearly do not know what they are talking about, and when somebody is trying to teach them the right way, these know-it-alls assume they have already mastered everything there is to know about that particular topic. In *their* minds, it is because it seems simple enough for them to understand and execute. How many times have you met a person to whom you are trying to tell them something important and they brush you off as though they know everything there is to know about that topic? And how many times do they miserably fail for not listening to your expert advice?

Turns out, this is quite a common thing. A lot of people who fail will have a level of overconfidence in their understanding, hence they might pay "less attention" to something important – because in *their* mind it is simply trivial. But as I told you before, the details are a treasure throve for manipulating tactics. Some of those details will seem imperceptive to most people, but there is that *"je ne se qua"* that makes something unique and different. For example, you might see a counterfeit garment which looks a lot like the original, but it is not until you put one side to side that you will be able to see the small differences and details that make an exclusive brand a lot more intricate that the counterfeit. There is value added to each detail. Some, as I said, might seem imperceptive, but for those who know what they are looking for, they will recognize the glaring differences.

For the willful ignorant, they might not want to know about these differences. They will either get said counterfeit garment knowing it is fake or get conned out of their money for buying something that is not real. Even if they got a "great deal" on said purchase. Of course, it is a "great deal" because it is fake. In other words, somebody made a fool of them because they did not know the difference. But for others, they might very well buy the counterfeit to try pass it as the real thing. And that in my humble opinion is a lot sadder. Why?

Because in the first instance, if a person gets swindled with a counterfeit – it is an instance of ignorance. But as I said, we all have blind spots. Maybe the person was familiar with the brand and the fact that it is exclusive - but that does not mean they have seen it up close or seen comparable legitimate models with their own eyes before. In other words, they did not quite know what to look for. And yes, exclusive brands tend to have a few easter- eggs that only those in the know would be able to find. Or at the very least there will be a certain level of craftsmanship needed, which is directly responsible for the higher value.

In the second instance, it is more about willful ignorance – and pretentiousness. In other words, is the person trying to deceive himself/herself or others? We know the adage, too many people spend money and they do not have to impress people they don't even like. And if their intent is to deceive, are they aware that somebody will be able to call them out on this being a fake product? For example, this might impress people who don't know any better. But for people who know better, they would look either like a person who got swindled, or a pretentious individual who is playing make believe. Also, if a person is knowingly brandishing something that is counterfeit, they will have a "story" if complimented on it. Either a real story about this not being the real deal or try to pretend this is indeed real. Neither of those are advisable. That is my humble view.

The reason is because this is another way to accept something misleading as a practical option. Personally, if there is something of a particular brand I care about – key words "care about" – then I will save enough to ensure I get the real deal after doing enough research to justify why I would acquire that something in the first place.

And why do I use the key words "care about?" Because not just because it is expensive or "exclusive" means that I need to have it, or that I want it for that matter. I will give you an example. I do not see myself buying a Rolex watch. Nothing wrong with this exclusive brand, but I cannot justify purchasing it, even though I could afford it. But just because I can afford it, that does not mean I need it or even want it. In my case I care more about functionality and usefulness. I do have a few "fancy" watches and wear them once in a while as garments – but none of them are anywhere near the cost of a Rolex. And to be honest, I do not even remember when the last time I got a chance to even wear any of the other fancy watches. For my day to day, I wear a Casio because it has the functionality and the usefulness I need on a day to day. And if needed be, I will wear one of the fancier watches for going out or something. What I will not do is buy a counterfeit Rolex and use it as a make believe. It is not so much about *who else* thinks it is real or not, it is the fact that *I know* that it is not real. Hence, trying to pretend does not play a role in my life, because I do not see the need, nor do I even want it in my case.

But let us use an example of something I do want. When it comes to musical instruments and gear, I do have an inclination for beauty and value. I have a collection of several high-end instruments such as real guitars from Gibson, Fender, Rickenbacker among others. There was research before each purchase, and in some instances, even though I could buy them outright at the sticker price I waited for a sale or any other opportunity to maximize the value. I would rather wait than go nuts.

Again, not just because you have the money within you means that you must burn a hole in your pocket. And now, if anybody compliments me about any of these instruments, I can give them the real story of each instrument with pride, and I can speak of the fact that I bought the real deal, and it was exactly what I wanted. And I can further point to the exact reasons why this purchase justified the wait and the expense.

Yes, there is a reason why I am drawing a parallel with these cited examples. When there is actual curiosity and research – and intellectual honesty, then you can find if what you want is indeed something that *you want* or if it is something that *you need*. But then again if you need it then you might as well get the actual thing you want. So logically your next decision will be showing the timeline to be given this desire. If it is urgent, then you might not be able to do much about it and get what you get – if it is for safety. But if you can and get what you like, need, and want, then wait until the right time. You will enjoy it more. I know I have. Every instrument I have gotten has a story and I enjoy playing them. Also, real exclusive items will have a better (or rather actual) resale value. A counterfeit, technically you are not supposed to re-sell it anyway because it is essentially fraud. Which means that you have spent money on something that is not even real and not worth its price tag anyway.

In life something similar happens. Many are choosing to willingly remain ignorant about something or the other – even though this could adversely affect them directly. And sadly, knowing more about it could be a mitigating factor to minimize or prevent something bad from happening in the first place. That is why I am saying, when we are willfully ignorant that gives tacit consent for somebody else to take control over our lives. And those taking control do not necessarily have *your* best interests in mind.

CHAPTER 6

HISTORICAL EXAMPLES |
The Evolution of Authoritarianism and Propaganda

There is no shortage of Authoritarian examples out there – we will focus on historical personalities, not so much the contemporary. Authoritarian regimes exist to this day. I will not be talking about those in this book. Why? Because I do not feel like getting shot in the face by an authoritarian who might feel it is justified to consider me a threat to their fragile ego for calling them out directly. All authoritarians we will cite in this chapter have one thing in common. They are all dead. Some of them died in incredibly savage ways. Although I will be quite thorough, I will not be digging too deep into each authoritarian figure cited. Mainly because this is by far the longest chapter in this book. Also, there is plenty of added biographical information on each, and I encourage you to learn more about them independently. It will help you enhance your critical thinking, and you will be able to expand on these patterns. Hopefully this will help you ascertain those indicators as you understand the world around you today. Remember, the lines on the map were not always drawn the way they are drawn today. And understanding the complexity of geopolitical facts is a big reason why I wrote this chapter in the manner that I did. Enjoy the ride.

This chapter is meant to illustrate how authoritarians have been among us since any semblance of civilized people started roaming the world. When I chose the personalities for this chapter, I also chose not to go too far back in history. Otherwise, it is human nature tending to be detached from these warnings as if these were happening only way back in the past. In other words, if most people might feel that something *happened back then*, then they would erroneously ascertain that it is no longer relevant to their world today.

As I mentioned before we will not be citing any contemporary authoritarian figures. A common denominator of authoritarians is that their gigantic egos are extremely fragile. They do not do well with criticism of any kind. That is why they tend to surround themselves by "yes men and women" exclusively. Any dissenting opinion tends to be terminated. Often in cruel and punitive ways.

Before we delve into the examples, I want to also draw a few other parallels for each case. Most of these authoritarian figures were officially elected. Yes, that means that people either voted for them, or otherwise and they rose to power legally. Others took power by ousting the previous regime. However, in those cases they had the support from enough people to continue their "revolution" and subsequently sediment their authoritarian powers. Also, and quite often, most people did not see the authoritarians coming into power necessarily as a bad thing. In fact, many of these authoritarian leaders were somehow populists. And of course, they all had a common enemy. They were against whatever establishment they were fighting at the time. Again, power is not just limited to the authoritarian figure but those who follow the authoritarian directives. In other words, turning rhetoric into action.

Another key part to their success, and unsurprisingly later demise for most authoritarian figures was the propaganda that helped them rise to power. When this propaganda lost its edge, then started working against them. Many authoritarians were brutally murdered by the very people they used to subjugate. Some of which were even their own authoritarian supporters at some point.

It really does not pay in the end to be an authoritarian leader, because there will come a moment in their regime where they cannot trust anybody. Their circle of trust will shrink and inevitably become an echo chamber. The closest advisors will not be providing actual guidance, but rather become a rubber stamp for whatever crazy paranoia is entering this authoritarian's head. And this phenomenon is not a matter of if, but when. Being an authoritarian is not sustainable, even if this authoritarianism goes through generations.

The examples I have cited in this chapter are in no chronological order. Also, some of these authoritarians likely still have a fan club behind their "legacy" – however destructive it might have been for humanity. Fortunately, the deceased authoritarian's fragile ego will not be further directly eroded by my words. All the following citations are biographical statements of fact, and they can be independently verified. Also, these are widely publicized, therefore there is no need for any sycophant to get offended by proxy for their departed *"dear leader."*

This list is non-inclusive. But it should give you a good starting point to understand that these ideologies can happen in every segment of our population. I had a long list of potential authoritarian options for this chapter. I chose the ones listed below because their combined histories relate to one another in some shape or form. I found this to be very helpful in order to balance the wide span of relevant factors to better illustrate my point. Also, most of these names are likely somebody you might have heard before, even if you are not familiar with the intricacies of their regime.

Benito Mussolini | Italy
Born 29 JUL 1883 – Died 28 APR 1945
Executed by firing squad.

Regime in power from 1922 to 1943

Benito Almicare Andrea Mussolini was born in Italy in the year of 1883. If you have ever heard the term "Fascist" when it comes to extreme right-wing political views – This is the person responsible for founding this extremist movement. Mussolini was Italy's Prime Minster during World War II (WWII) when Italy was aligned with Nazi Germany during this conflict.

Several decades before WWII, Mussolini grew up in a household where his father was an ardent Socialist (left-wing in the political spectrum), and his mother was a very devoted Catholic. His father was a blacksmith and was very much devoted to politics *and* his mistress. Yes, he was unfaithful to Mussolini's mother. Mussolini's mother was a teacher, and she was holding the household afloat. Mussolini was the oldest of three children. Mussolini was known for his remarkable intelligence, but he was also extremely disobedient and quite the troublemaker at school. His father was the catalyst for Mussolini's initial interest in Socialism and defiance against authority. Unsurprisingly, this defiance and harassment against school authorities and classmates caused Mussolini to be expelled from several schools throughout his life. Surprisingly enough, he got an education certificate in 1901 and was a school master for a little while.

In 1902 he moved to Switzerland where he expanded his socialist views. The Swiss authorities did not appreciate that type of rhetoric, and Mussolini was forced to return to Italy in 1904 where he continued promoting Socialist agendas. Despite being briefly imprisoned, he started to work as an editor of the *"Avanti"* (moving forward) Socialist newspaper. This gigantic platform helped him to become a more influential man. Mussolini was against Italy entering World War I (WWI) in the beginning. But he later changed his mind and supported the war in order to "Make Italy Great Again." This put him at odds with the people in the Socialist party and he was ejected from that organization. Mussolini joined the Army in 1915, where he rose to the rank of Corporal and was discharged after being wounded in the front lines.

Finally, on March 23, 1919, Mussolini founded the extreme right-wing Fascist Party. This party's rhetoric was supposed to be a way to capitalize on the greatness of the former Roman Empire. To this end he united several right-wing groups under the same umbrella. This movement was touted as fostering nationalist sentiments and breaking social class oppression. This nationalistic pride was also full of Roman symbology that created a visceral response in people.

For example, the "fascism" term is derived as a "light" or "torch" used by ancient Romans.

Of course, this Fascist movement acted in heavy opposition to the incumbent Italian government. In fact, Mussolini used terminology that described the incumbent government as weak. Mussolini created the "Black Shirts" paramilitary unit that was intended to terrorize his political opposition. Because the treaty of Versailles was not good news for Italy, there was plenty of public discontent with the government. Mussolini and his followers took advantage of this situation to rally support.

By this time Mussolini had quite the name recognition and touted as though he was the only one who could restore order in the country. Mussolini became Prime Minister in 1922. In just a few years in 1925 he became Italy's Dictator and assumed the name of *"Il Duce"* which means "The Leader." Unsurprisingly, by then he had dismantled any entities or organizations that could be a threat to his power. Despite his exceedingly egotistical and ruthlessly violent power grab, he was able to raise employment and that was an effective way to rally support. Another thing he did was give a lot of credence to the Catholic Church to gain their support, and the support from their congregation. Mussolini was an atheist himself, but it is understood that he was so egotistical that he would have considered *himself* a deity. In either case, Mussolini was interested in expanding the Italian Empire under his name to galvanize his personal legacy.

One of the ways he figured he could achieve that was by invading Ethiopia in 1935. Ethiopia was an easy target and was unable to compete against the superior Italian military equipment at the time. This country was easily appropriated under this Italian Empire and help him boast about his military prowess. In 1939 Mussolini sent Fascist troops to help Franco in Spain fight during the Spanish Civil War.

Adolf Hitler was very impressed with Mussolini's track record. It has been said that Mussolini was not *that* impressed by Hitler at first, but Mussolini was quite impressed years after when he saw the support Hitler was able to rally by capitalizing on many of Mussolini's lessons. Hitler from the start knew how to stroke Mussolini's ego and was able get Italy to become their ally. In 1939 both dictators signed what is known as the "Pact of Steel," and that led him to adopt some of Hitler's discriminating policies that were central in WWII, such as de-facto crimes against humanity. Among these were the deportations of Jewish people and other groups into concentration camps and other summary executions. In 1940 Italy invaded Greece without much trouble in the onset. Once Germany invaded Poland WWII started for Italy, which meant that Italy was siding with Germany against the rest of Europe and America, minus the neutral countries, such as Switzerland or Spain.

For example, Franco declined to enter WWII because among other things, Spain was still spent from the Spanish Civil War. During WWII Italy fought against the rest of the most powerful allied forces in the world which included the United States of America, Great Britain, and the Soviet Union. Sometime during 1941, Hitler's military saved Mussolini from being ousted in a coup after many military setbacks.

It was not until a few years later that the allied forces took the Italian peninsula after entering through Sicily. Mussolini was forced to resign on July 25, 1943. Unsurprisingly Mussolini was arrested, but once again the German military came to the rescue and helped him escape. Mussolini tried to reestablish his government in the northern part of Italy to no avail. Rome was finally liberated from Mussolini by allied forces on June 4, 1944. On April 27, 1945, Mussolini tried to escape to Switzerland with his mistress. They both got captured and executed on April 28, 1945, in the city of Mezzegra by the Italian underground. Their bodies were put on display in a plaza in Milan.

Italians were happy to be liberated from this dictator who brought so much pain and suffering. Mussolini was always looking after himself. Anything he did was to primarily satisfy his ego while exploiting people's biases, recruiting them as loyal followers, and deceive them in order to be able to enact an extremist agenda. Mussolini's method has been copied by several authoritarians throughout history.

---***** ---

Augusto Pinochet | Chile
Born 25 NOV 1915 – Died 10 DEC 2006
Died of a heart attack while in house arrest in a Santiago, Chile hospital.

Regime in power 1973 to 1990

Augusto José Ramón Pinochet Ugarte was born in Chile 1915. He ascended into power after betraying the very person who helped him climb through the ranks and gain a position of prominence in Chile. Regardless of the brutality his regime enacted, he was *loved* by many Chileans, and even admired by First-World Leaders who considered Pinochet a *friend*. Goes to tell you how complex the geopolitical situation and the minds of everyday people can become based on a bias under several factors and metrics.

Pinochet was born into a middle-class family in Valparaiso, Chile. His mother was deeply religious, and Pinochet was very much attached to his mother; not so much with his father. Pinochet was not a good student growing up; despite the fact that he attended prestigious institutions. He was considered good at art, but regardless he was subjected to bullying by his peers. They even nicknamed him derogatorily as "the donkey" (*el burro*). An allusion to the fact he was not very smart as a student. "*Burro*" in Spanish is also being used as a euphemism for "dumb." Pinochet decided he was going to become a solider, despite the fact his father was hoping for him to become a doctor. In either case Pinochet's application to join the military was denied numerous times. Somehow it was due to his mother's persistence that Pinochet was finally able to join the military in

1933. Once in uniform he was not a particularly proficient military man either.

This part of his military tenure was during WWII and the beginnings of the Cold War. Therefore, there was no shortage of Communists trying to make South America their home. Pinochet oversaw an outpost for the detainment of Communists in the country. This is where he met the person who would be somewhat intertwined with the rest of his legacy – Salvador Allende, who was a Marxist. After many trials and tribulations, Allende later became the democratically elected leader of Chile in 1973. However, this being during the Cold War era, the West – particularly the US under the Nixon administration – was not ok at all with a Socialist being in power, let alone a full-blown Communist. Therefore, they wanted to oust Allende by evoking a coup also in 1973. Before 1970, years earlier, the West tried to diminish Allende's influence. This effort backfired miserably and instead it unified the country of Chile to rally behind Allende. Yes, even those who did not particularly care about Allende supported him. That is why leaders must be careful when attacking another country's "National Pride."

While all this was happening, Pinochet who was a very unremarkable military leader, somehow landed the job as Commander of a Garrison in Chile's capital, Santiago. When this coup was attempted, Pinochet defended Allende from being ousted. At the time the highest-ranking member of the Chilean Armed Forces, General Carlos Prats, was so impressed with Pinochet's response that he even recommended Allende to give Pinochet his spot as the Chilean Armed Forces highest-ranking officer. This came as surprise to many because Pinochet was better known as an underachiever. After Prats left his position, a few other Chilean generals approached Pinochet and told him that essentially, they were going to conduct a coup, and that Pinochet was welcome to participate, and if he did not want to join it was going to happen anyway.

Remember, at this point Pinochet was appointed the exulted title of Commander in Chief of the Army by Salvador Allende. Regardless,

Pinochet betrayed Allende this time as he agreed to be part of the plot to overthrow him in 1973. The country woke up on September 11, 1973, to military planes and military equipment attacking the *"Palacio de la Moneda"* in Chile's capital Santiago. In an ironic turn of events Allende was worried about Pinochet's safety, not knowing that he was behind this attack. Allende committed suicide during the coup by shooting himself. Interesting fact, the suicide gun Allende used was a gift from Cuban Dictator Fidel Castro. Allende was of course a disciple of Castro and Marxist principles.

Pinochet took power over the county and started a macabre campaign by killing any left-leaning people in the country. His targets even included artists and intellectuals aside from political enemies. Pinochet directed his followers to conduct summary executions in public places such as stadiums. Behind closed doors, he would have the daughters of political enemies being used as subjects for torture and even forced to have intercourse with animals for the amusement of some deprived soldiers. The executions also happened abroad. For example, Prats was killed in a car bomb in Argentina and other oppositions leaders were killed even in the relative safety of Washington D.C.

Despite these atrocities, there were many Chileans who were infatuated with Pinochet and would turn a blind eye to any justified criticism. Primarily because Pinochet was able to rescue the country's economy after years of decline. Many of those declined economic trends were attributed to Allende's policies, as he was unable to control the most radical left-leaning segments from his party. Pinochet's plan, although risky, made Chile one of the richest countries in South America and the world. There was no one to stop him, Pinochet gained unilateral power by essentially killing any person who had a dissenting opinion. Pinochet continued pressing for referendums to keep himself in power. He was able to enact changes in the constitution and it worked until 1988 when the people voted him out. He left office in 1990. However, on his way out of office he appointed himself once again as Commander in Chief of the Army.

He held that post until 1998 and granted himself immunity against any prosecution. Yes, this enabled him to avoid justice despite all his crimes against humanity. He lived a comfortable and relatively carefree life.

It was not until 1998 when he was in London for a medical intervention that he was arrested by crimes committed against Spanish citizens. These crimes would call for extradition, but there was a lot of controversy to protect Pinochet from answering to this allegation. Even right-wing figure Margaret Thatcher, who was the United Kingdom's Prime Minister at the time, defended him. This was under the guise that Pinochet was in bad health to stand trial. He spent some time on house arrest in the UK, but then he flew back to Santiago where he defiantly stood up from his wheelchair once he was on safe land after avoiding justice. Subsequently, renewed cases surfaced and required Pinochet to answer for these crimes against humanity. In 2004 Chile revoked his immunity and he was finally going to face justice for these crimes against humanity. However, he died in 2006 before he could be tried for his crimes and there were hundreds of other prosecutions for people who perpetrated crimes in support of his regime.

This is an interesting case, because the people in Chile are still divided when it comes to Pinochet. He is an example of how an unremarkable person in the right place at the right time could change the course of history. In this case, he influenced an entire country despite the fact he was regularly an underachiever. However, he was ruthless, and his followers perpetrated heinous crimes against humanity. What is even worse, is that despite the fact he was to be prosecuted, Pinochet died before being tried for his crimes. Regardless, his legacy will remain as a dictator who perpetrated crimes against humanity.

*****

Mobutu Sese Seko | Zaire (Democratic Republic of Congo)
Born 14 OCT 1930 – Died 07 SEP 1997
Died of prostate cancer.

Regime in power from 1965 to 1997

Mobutu Sese Seko Kuku Ngbendu Wa Za Banga (also known as Joseph Desire Mobutu) was born in Belgian Congo in 1930. The Republic of Congo though was gaining freedom from colonist's European rule, eventually fell into the corrupt hands of their new dictator Mobutu Sese Seko. He was a former journalist turned Army Officer. He is an example of corruption empowered by unaccounted power. He rose to fame, not surprisingly, as a populist. And building this enticement to the populace would not have been exceedingly difficult at the time, because being under Belgian's rule life was brutal for this colony if you had dark skin. Mobutu Sese Seko was born out of wedlock, and largely unacknowledged by his birth father.

Although Congo had gained independence, the ruling class was formed of white European descent and incredibly racist.

Mobutu Sese Seko figured that he could use this system to his advantage and moved to join the *Force Publique* in the capital serving under this ruling class. He achieved the highest rank available to Black people at the time, which was sergeant. But he was also a journalist, and this is the part that resonated the most with his people. Being the 1950's there was quite the trend of decolonization around the world. The Belgians left this colony when they realized they could not govern this gigantic country. On June 30, 1960, this "Belgian Congo" colony became the Democratic Republic of Congo.

At this point Mobutu Sese Seko gained a high position in the Armed Forces and National Defense. Although independent, this new republic was anything but stable. This instability led to civil war. These events occurred during the time of the Cold War; therefore, superpowers were very interested in the outcome of this event. A series of political confrontations occurred which included coup attempts. With all these divergences his time finally arrived on November 24, 1965. He had the army suspend democracy to "temporarily" give unilateral power to Mobutu Sese Seko.

This was not the first time this "temporary" suspension of democracy had happened. He acted in a similar fashion a few years prior to this event and that time he gave power back. Of course, this precedent gave a false sense of security to the population. But this time both leaders who were at odds when this suspension of government occurred happened to die under mysterious circumstances. One of them was even confined to house arrest right after Mobutu Sese Seko seized power. Mobutu Sese Seko of course blamed partisanship and banned any journalistic efforts in the country. All these dissenters became scapegoats for any instability.

All parties were then turned in to the "Popular Movement of the Revolution" – this became mandatory for every citizen. In other words, when the elections came, Mobutu Sese Seko became the leader because there were no other parties. This of course gave him unilateral power and led to one of the most corrupt dictatorships in history. Many historians will characterize his regime as a "kleptocracy." He became a tyrant very quickly; he held had public executions by hanging political enemies in a stadium. This spree of killings even included previous allies who were no longer needed by him. Torture and sexual violence became commonplace tools for oppression. He wanted to create his "authentic" sense of leadership akin to hyperbolic depictions of a tribe chief who would have exuberant wealth and power. This type of governing was of course in contrast to what most Western or European democracies would dictate. Again, he used this rationale under the guise of "authenticity" to galvanize his power. He banned essentially anything that would have Western influence, to include music.

He collected all kinds of properties and would even take flights for shopping whenever he pleased. He was born in a small village called Gbadolite. This small village was barely known or even mapped. During his rule he turned this place into a five- star town, he tore down all the old village and constructed a luxury town. He even put runways large enough for concord planes to take-off and land. He also made a palace known as the "Versailles of the Jungle." Of course, that excess was happening even though his nation was not rich, but that did not matter to him. His excesses continued sinking the population deeper into destitution.

The way he was able to do this was by exploiting the nation's natural resources but using cronies to get away with this process. He has been quoted saying "everything is for sale; anything can be bought in our country." And of course, that means that many countries would turn a blind eye to these citizen abuses, so long they could get access to these mineral riches; which included among other things diamonds, and rare-earth metals. He then changed the country's name to "Zaire;" and renamed himself to Mobutu Sese Seko Kuku Ngebendu Waza Banga which means "The all-powerful warrior who because of his endurance and inflexible will to win will go from conquest to conquest leaving fire in his wake."

As previously mentioned, his regime was occurring during Cold War times, therefore it was not unusual for the superpowers to turn blind eye to atrocities if this meant that the adversary would not get influence over these unsavory world leaders first. In 1975 Zaire sent troops against Angola, and Angola beat the crap out of them.

In 1973 "Zaireanization" was enacted to expropriate foreign interests and nationalization of foreign business. Of course, this backfired because the cronies did not have the same business chops as those who were sideswiped by Mobutu Sese Seko. In 1980, economic power made it a lot more comfortable for this dictator. Mobutu Sese Seko also slept with several of his cronies' wives to humiliate them, just to show his power. However, his power was far from absolute. There were a lot of other conspirators working behind the scenes giving him the <u>illusion he was in charge</u>. That was until things started to get harder as the money became tight.

As the Soviet Union collapsed, then western nations started to assert their disdain for this country and then distanced themselves from this dictator. The West was giving aid to Zaire when the Soviet Union was a threat, but once the Soviet Union collapsed, the money also stopped in the 1990's. Inflation peaked at 7,000% in Zaire, but Mobutu Sese Seko was not worried about that – himself. He just moved to his palace and basked in luxury while the rest of the country suffered.

A civil war killed 800,000 people (about half the population of Idaho) in the neighboring country of Rwanda. Mobutu Sese Seko tried to gain favor with the West by opening Zaire to refugees, but a lot of those people mixed with the refugees were also part of the genocidal group responsible for those crimes. On July 4, 1994, the Rwandan Patriotic Front (RPF) made it to the capital and toppled the government of the neighboring country of Rwanda. Zaire was then a staging ground to continue this civil war massacre inside this neighboring country.

By this time, Mobutu Sese Seko has become incontinent with prostate cancer in 1996. The RPF of course by now has moved to take over Zaire by training a Zairian rebel group. There was a coalition of African states that Mobutu Sese Seko had burned bridges in the past. When Mobutu Sese Seko returned to try to defend his regime, very few people were willing to give their lives for this sick man.

The rebels fought all over the country. Mobutu Sese Seko begged the West for help, but the West was not willing to aid this despotic dictator. Mobutu Sese Seko used his plane to flee into exile as bullets hit the aircraft. The plane was refused to land in many countries. Eventually the only country willing to accept him was Morocco.

He died in Morocco as his palace was looted and the country was renamed as the Democratic Republic of Congo. His legacy left a minerally rich country in instability and destitution.

*****

Hugo Chávez | Venezuela
Born 28 JUL 1954 – Died 05 MAR 2013
Died of cancer.

Regime in power from 1999 to 2013

Hugo Rafael Chávez Frías was born in Venezuela 1954. Both his parents were teachers. Yet him and his family grew up in poverty and faced firsthand the inequality that existed in Venezuela. This is yet another case of a person who rose to prominence as a product of his environment. Although Chavez is different than other leaders in this list in the sense that he is not *directly* accused of committing crimes against humanity; his influence opened the door to other radicalized groups that created an unsustainable paradigm after he was gone. Case in point, Venezuela has not been able to recover from the economic crisis that occurred after his death. And his at-the-time Vice President, Nicolás Maduro, never achieved the level of success that Chavez enjoyed. Regardless of if you agree or disagree with Chavez' policies, he was very smart and shrewd. This does not necessarily mean that otherwise "good intentions" will translate to sustainable opportunities for his constituents.

Let us explore the timeline of significant events leading to his rise to power.

In 1971 Chavez enrolled in the Caracas Venezuelan Academy of Military Sciences. He graduated four years later top of his class. However, he was always opinionated and even though he was in uniform he was known for sowing ideas that were very much aligned with extreme-left doctrines, even though they were not officially recognized by the military. For example, in 1977 he started the Venezuela's People's Liberation Army. Subsequently in 1982 he started the Bolivarian Revolutionary Army, which was later known as the Revolutionary Bolivarian Movement-200 (MBR-200).

While serving in uniform Chavez would teach the troops his Bolivarian Revolutionary ideas. In his assertion, the country, and the Armed Forces themselves were corrupt and flawed. Of course, that got him in trouble, yet he still advanced in rank. Nonetheless, he was the head of a failed coup on February 4, 1992. Chavez was arrested and persuaded to give the names of the people who helped him. He showed up on TV wearing his military uniform and when he was about to give the names of those who helped him, instead he mentioned "Simón Bolivar" who is better known as the liberator of [South] America from the colonial Spanish Crown power. Chavez was in prison until 1994 but because of this stunt, he gained a cult following that exists to this day. Also, on his favor, Venezuela's bad economy, rampant corruption and extreme inequality fostered an environment where he could push his message. He then created the *Fifth Republic Movement and* was elected with a 56% margin on February 2, 1999. Gaining populous support, especially from those Venezuelans who were disenfranchised under previous administrations, he was able to galvanize his power. Most people would see him as the savior of the country. He was "one of them" – giving voice and resources to those who were otherwise destitute in earlier administrations.

Let us now explore how this galvanization of power was used as a way to entice democratically driven populist votes.

Chavez even renamed the country to "Bolivarian Republic of Venezuela." During his first term he used a more capitalistic approach but amended the constitution in his favor. Venezuela did improve during his first term with these moderate policies. Unsurprisingly, he got reelected with almost 60% of the vote. Things started to change in his Second term. Chavez who was a disciple of Fidel Castro got closer to Cuba during this period. And of course, this started the trend of Venezuela distancing from the United States. Chavez nationalized major portions of Venezuela's oil reserves, making it one of the primary sources of income to support Chavez' social programs. Chavez also nationalized a lot of other industries. This populist segmentation was instrumental on his third reelection, although with a smaller margin than on his second term.

This time for Chavez it was about the "Bolivarian Alliance" push. To understand the context of this principle, we need to go well before the time Chavez rose to power. There is something known as the *"El Sueño de Bolivar"* or roughly translated to "Simón Bolivar Dream;" which was Bolivar's vision of having Latin American countries linked as a great unification of nations working together as one. Much like the United States of America (USA), or to a lesser extent the European Union (EU). That did not happen, every country went on and did their own thing after being liberated from Spain. Bolivar died brokenhearted and sick after helping fight so many years in the name of freedom and independence. This part of history is a lot more complex, but rather than taking too long to dissect every aspect, I want to emphasize that a significant driver on the rhetoric was based on this principle as I described.

Fast forward several scores after Bolivar's death but <u>well before</u> Chavez' rise to power, the *"Pacto Andino"* which roughly translates to the Andes Pact started to get some traction. This was an idea that floated about uniting the countries which are part of the Andes Mountain range. In a way, much like the USA or perhaps like the EU. Well, at the time Chile and Venezuela were not really onboard with that. Mostly because *their* economies were great and the rest of the countries not so much. If the *"Pacto Andino"* would have come to fruition it would have made Chile, Bolivia, Peru, Ecuador, Colombia, and Venezuela a mega country of sorts, or at least a huge customs- free trade zone. I can write an entire book about that topic alone, but I will leave it at that because the point to all this historical background is that it gave very distinctively visceral responses to a lot of people in the region. I remember when I was a kid hearing so much about it. And the *for and against* contentions were pretty heated up among the "grown-ups."

Chavez' idealistic far-left principles rallied the support of many like-minded presidents. All of which were not aligned with the USA. Chavez influenced many other countries who had potential for very extreme-left leaning politics. In fact, some of those countries were authoritarian. These regimes were welcoming whomever who had rhetoric that misaligned with the United States. For example, by calling the West or USA as *"el Imperio Yankee"* or the Yankee

Empire." This opened the door to a lot of division between the individual populations themselves and a separation at the larger geopolitical level.

However, many people in each of those countries would not quite understand the repercussions that their support to Chavez' ideology could create onto themselves and the region at large. Even if the policies had some sort of *populist-equalizer*... they are not sustainable. But that is a much more complex strata I will write an entire book about. But for now, we will call for the common denominator. Unintended consequences.

Based on this populism Chavez was reelected for a fourth term in 2012. By this time, Chavez was very ill and had to postpone the inauguration. His Vice President, Nicolás Maduro took over Chavez' seat. In 2011 Chavez was diagnosed with cancer, he had three surgeries to try to remove tumors, but Chavez ultimately succumbed to cancer in 2013. Maduro was a bus driver before his rise in politics. This of course helped Chavez prove to the Venezuelan population that *anybody who had enough patriotism* could be afforded an opportunity to raise to a position of high prestige and power. Unfortunately for Venezuela, where Chavez was an extraordinary orator and highly capable politician, Maduro hit a perfect storm when the price of oil dropped, and with that the Venezuelan economy declined overnight, and inflation skyrocketed.

However, the damage extended way further than Venezuela. Many minds across the nations friendly to Chavez had been misinformed and radicalized. And because Venezuela and other countries became extreme left, it is a reason why a lot of expats from these countries tend to be very much right-leaning, or even trending to the extreme-right. That is why a divisive figure can enact exponential unintended consequences, even reaching far away from their own lands.

*****

Fidel Castro | Cuba
Born 13 AUG 1926 – Died 25 NOV 2016
Died of natural causes.

Regime in power from 1958 to "2008" (2016 technically)

Fidel Alejandro Castro Ruz was born in Cuba 1926. He is known as the longest-in-power dictator from Cuba (yes there has been more than one). Even though he passed away in 2016, as his health was declining Fidel Castro conceded the power onto his brother Raúl Castro over Cuba in 2008. Fidel Castro is one of the most influential dictators, and many other authoritarians and *authoritarian-lite* regimes were set up based on Castro's doctrines. Castro rose to power by organizing the revolution that ousted the previous Cuban dictator Fulgencio Batista. Cuba is still under dictatorial rule at the time I am typing this manuscript.

As Castro gained power he instituted a Communist system, and aligned Cuba with the Soviet Union. This of course strained and then destroyed relationships with the United States after the 1962 Cuban Missile Crisis. This is when the Soviet Union was getting nuclear missiles to be aimed at the United States mainland from Cuba. Cuba is less than 100 miles from Florida.

Domestically, Castro improved healthcare and education, but like most dictators he would prosecute, imprison and in many cases execute, any person with dissenting opinions. Thousands have died trying to flee this regime. The United States of America (USA) imposed an embargo in Cuba, the Castro regime depended in great part on the Soviet Union's support. When the Soviet Union collapsed in the 90's, Castro had no choice but to relax some of the stringent rules in the country, but the country remained highly authoritarian. Even when his brother Raúl was taking over the country in 2008, Fidel Castro would still wield power from the sidelines until he passed away at the age of 90 in 2016.

Fidel Castro's father was a wealthy sugar plantation owner from Spain. Fidel was born out of wedlock, and it was not until he was 17 that his father married his mother. Fidel then changed his last name from Ruz to Castro. Castro went to boarding school and educational institutions of high prestige. He was known to be a good student, but a troublemaker. Also, he was very much into sports and athletic endeavors. As he went into law school, he was immersed in socialist views, politics, anti- imperialism, Cuban-nationalism, etc.

His revolutionary career started in 1947 when he started taking part in the failed coup inside the Dominican Republic and antigovernment demonstrations in Colombia. In the same year he joined an anti-communist group led by Eduardo Chibas, this led nowhere having Chibas' shooting himself while giving a radio broadcast. Around that time Castro married and this marriage gave him a lot more political influence. Castro was going to run for Congress, but then in 1952 Batista rose to power by organizing a coup. Therefore, the next election was cancelled and left Castro in a dire economic situation to sustain his family.

Batista was aligned with the military and the elites, and his regime was recognized by the United States. Castro attempted the first coup against Batista on July 26, 1953, with about 150 men. He failed, got arrested and sentenced to 15 years in prison. While in prison, he started planning the revolution. Eventually with got released in 1955 thanks to an amnesty deal. Him and his brother Raúl who were imprisoned together moved to Mexico to continue planning the revolution.

In Mexico, Castro met with other people in exile, and this included the infamous Argentinian Ernesto "Che" Guevara. Guevara was convinced that Latin people should take arms and use violence to justify any perceived wrongdoing that was done to poor people. Guevara joined the Castro brothers in the revolution and became Fidel's confidant. At the end of 1956 Castro along with 80 insurgents and weapons returned to Cuba. Batista was able to kill and capture a large group of these dissidents. Fidel Castro, Raúl, and "Che" Guevara were able to escape and started to recruit people around the Sierra Nevada and the southwestern coast for the next couple of years. During this time, they gained large amounts of support, established a parallel government helping certain communities, and of course conducted guerrilla warfare against Batista's forces.

In 1958 Castro has successfully gained control over certain key areas of Cuba. Batista's power was dwindling and that included a lot of desertion from his own military forces. Batista end up fleeing the country to the Dominican Republic. Castro gained control over the revolution in January 1959 at age 32. However, it was José Miro Cardona who became the new president, while Castro was the Commander in Chief of the Military. In 1959 Miro resigned and Castro became Prime Minister. While all this was taking place hundreds of Batista's government members were executed.

Castro then instated Communist rules despite telling the United States that they were not Communist. The country nationalized essentially everything, provided rations to the citizens, and started buying at low price anything that was owned by the United States. Castro realized that many American landowners have artificially lowered the price of lands and industries in order to have a lower tax liability. Unsurprisingly this strained relations with the United States. So much so that the United States President Eisenhower declined meeting with Castro when he visited America. Castro retaliated by signing an agrarian reform that limited property ownership by foreign entities. Of course, this was done under the guise of giving opportunities to the Cuban farmers. But it was a tool to control the populace and by extension their agricultural production. Any dissenting opinions were met with violence, or by being forced out of the country, and/or getting executed. This punishment was awarded to civilians and the military.

Another thing that occurred was the censoring of any media in Cuba, especially anything critical against the regime. In 1960 Cuba signed a trade agreement with the Soviet Union (USSR). This among other factors created even more tension between USA and Cuba. On January 3, 1961, Eisenhower broke relation with the Cuban government. John F. Kenny was the incoming American president, and he inherited the Bay of Pigs fiasco in April 1961. A coup to overthrow Castro was planned under the Eisenhower administration, but Kennedy did not supply air support to the rebels in order to conceal the fact that the United States had any involvement. Of course, the rebel forces got massacred and this helped Castro sediment his power. On May of the same year, Castro put an end to any attempt to democratic elections in Cuba and named the USA as an imperialist country. Subsequently, Castro appointed himself a Marxist-Leninist and fully imposed Communist rules and policies onto the Cuban people. On February 7, 1962, the United States imposed the full embargo onto Cuba that is still to this day (the time I am writing this book).

Later in October 1962 Castro wanting to garnish more support from the Soviet Union, agreed with the at-the-time Soviet leader Nikita Khrushchev to place missiles in Cuba. This was a tit-for- tat as the United States had missiles in Turkey. Kennedy was able to gain intelligence that the missiles were going to be placed in Cuba and ordered the U.S. Navy to search any vessel coming towards Cuba. In the end, secret meetings between Kennedy and Khruschev reached an agreement to remove the missiles from both places. Castro was left out of the negotiations by both governments, leaving him ostracized from the rest of the international community as it almost led the world into nuclear Armageddon. Credit to both American and Soviet leaders at the time for their restrain. Otherwise, the world would have likely ended <u>that</u> year in radioactive vapor.

There is plenty more to talk about Fidel Castro and his brutal regime. Therefore, I am going to end here and move on to the next authoritarian. But the point I wanted to drive with this recount is the fact that an authoritarian can put in jeopardy the entire world. Obviously, the people under the authoritarians are suffering, but this is normally a consequence of a façade that is portrayed as originally benevolent. I would be remiss if I did not mention that external governments also miscalculated and made glaring mistakes that exacerbate the problem as it pertains to Cuba. And that is yet another reason why I wanted to point out how authoritarianism at the macro level can be so complex and abstract in principle.

Castro's doctrines are overreaching, and this "revolutionary" influence has spanned several countries around the world. Many authoritarians have become his disciples. Either directly or by proxy. Castro's legacy of division continues to this day, even though he has been dead for several years. That is why it is so dangerous. A lot of figures such as the "Che Guevara" get romanticized, but the truth is a lot darker. That is why understanding history in context is so important.

---------- ***** ----------

Joseph Stalin | Soviet Union
Born 18 DEC 1878 – Died 05 MAR 1953
Died of hemorrhagic stroke.

Regime in power from 1924 to 1953

Ioseb Besarionis dze Jughashvili was born in the Russian Empire, present day Georgia 1878. Stalin was in power for over two decades, he was one of the most ruthless authoritarians in world history. Even though he was instrumental in defeating the Nazis during World War II (WWII), his regime was riddle with incompetence, destruction, famine, among many other exponentially damaging policies that superseded his death.

However, the *"Man of Steel"* (Stalin) was actually a very different person as a child. When Stalin was seven years old, he contracted smallpox leaving his face scared, and later he suffered an accident which left his left arm with a minor deformity. He grew up in a humble home with his parents having simple jobs. Kids in his village treated him with cruelty, and paired with these other physical hindrances Stalin developed an inferiority complex.

However, this rage worsened a fervent desire for respect, and power. As a result, he became cruel to anybody who crossed him. As 1888 came about, Stalin's mother who was a fervent Russian Orthodox Christian pushed him to enroll in seminar to become a priest. He was accepted to the Tiflis Theological Seminary in 1894. In 1895 Stalin learned about a secret organization that advocated for Georgian independence from Russia. He joined this group in 1898. For context, around this point in time the Russian monarchy was still in power. This group Stalin joined was called the Messame Dassy and featured writings from Marx and Lenin.

He left the seminary school in 1899, even though he was a very good student. There is disagreement among historians saying that he was either unable to pay the tuition or that he was separated because of his political views against Tsar Nicholas II. Personally, I would not be surprised if it was part of both. It is very likely that Stalin was very vocal about his political views and coming from humble roots it would have been hard to make ends meet. The wealth gap when the Tsar was in power was also very stark indeed.

In 1901 Stalin chose to spend all his time with the revolutionary movement, as he joined the Social Democratic Labor Party, whist working full time for the revolutionary movement whose goal was to outs the monarch.

In 1902 Stalin was arrested for the first time after coordinating a labor strike. He was punished and sent to Siberia. He was indeed arrested and exiled several other times. That is when he changed his name to "Stalin" which translates to "steel" in Russian. Around this time, he was also very much inside Lenin's circle of trust and became an insider to the overall group's cadre.

Stalin was never as charismatic or eloquent as Lenin was, but Stalin was quite good at administrative tasks that ranged from publishing propaganda leaflets to organizing strikes and demonstrations. After Stalin escaped from exile, he was wanted by the Tsar's secret police. Stalin raised money through criminal activities that included kidnapping, extorsion, and robberies. That included the 1907 Tiflis bank robbery where he got the equivalent of 3.4 million U.S. Dollars or about 250,000 rubles on that time's money. The violence enacted during this heist added to his notoriety.

As February 1917 rolled around, the Russian Revolution started, and by the very next month the monarch was placed in house arrest. Although the revolutionaries at first supported the provisional government Lenin did not trust them, and in April 1917 Lenin had taken control by positioning the Bolsheviks to appoint himself as the leader. Lenin finally took full control of the government by October of the same year. But before that, Lenin had already taken possession of the land and factories from the rich and the industrialists around the country.

Unsurprisingly, there was a power struggle between those outside of government and between those inside this new government. Various figures were working with their own selfish interests in mind to gain control and power. Stalin was one of those people. In 1922 Stalin was given the title as General Secretary for the new Communist Party. This was not a very powerful office on its own right but gave Stalin control over all party member appointments.

This was a phenomenal networking opportunity as he was able to gain loyalist based on their own selfish desires, or by placing people in roles that would be helpful to him. Of course, he made it clear to these party members to acknowledge that their placement and access was thanks to him directly. This happened under Lenin nose, and by the time he got wind of that, Stalin was already well established. By this time, Lenin was very much frustrated with Stalin and his tactics, as well as the way the party had become increasingly corrupt against their supposed ideology of fairness towards all citizens. Lenin's health had been in rapid decline which aggravated the situation. Lenin died knowing that Stalin was going to be in power of the Soviet Union against his (Lenin's) own wishes.

When Lenin passed away in 1924 the obvious occurred, Stalin destroyed the old party's leadership and took unilateral control. At first, he used bureaucracy and other administrative means to denounce and in some instance shift positions. But soon enough he started his reign of terror. His paranoia grew as many of his political dissidents were exiled to America and Europe. He started arresting people in the middle of the night and put them through spectacular trails to set a dark example to anyone who dared to dissent against him. Anybody who was a potential rival was targeted and labeled "enemy of the people." These verdicts of course led to summary executions in what came to be known as the "Great Purge." This was not only limited to political enemies, it extended to any officials suspected of dissent. And of course, Stalin was also against anyone who had a favorable view of capitalist nations. Being revolutionary himself, Stalin viciously targeted anybody who would be a counter revolutionary.

As Stalin was able to violently get rid of anybody who voiced dissent, he started to push his own agenda. Between the late 1920s and early 1930's he reversed the Bolshevik agrarian policy. This was the policy Lenin intended to give the peasants some land so they could make a living that was fairer, instead of the – in essence – indented servitude under the Tsars. Stalin reversed this very principle that rallied support for the Russian revolution and turned the peasants back into serfs, except that this time it was by instituting collective farms.

In his mind, Stalin found that collectivism would accelerate food production. But of course, he did not consider the human factor. The peasants were not happy about losing their land and working for the state at bargain price to meet arbitrary quotas. The collective farming of course failed miserably and caused millions to die of starvation in one of the worst famines in the world's history. Pair this with forced labor and this was obviously unsustainable. Of course, these communal farms were portrayed in propaganda as great success stories. Even other like-minded nations such as Communist China under Mao copied this model – which of course resulted in their own catastrophic famine.

Stalin also started accelerated industrialization, which at the start seemed very promising. But much like the agricultural plan, this was simply not sustainable. Unsafe and inefficient factories and industries damaged the environment exponentially, and of course cost millions of lives throughout the Soviet Republics. Also, they had to be heavily subsided by the government. People knew better than to speak their discontent, as they would be taken to the Gulags for forced labor or being immediately executed. The rank structure in the party created a paradigm of "Yes men and women." If you spoke out of turn against the party, or even a person slightly higher ranking than you in the party your life and the lives of anyone you loved could be terminated in a brutal manner in no time.

By this time World War II (WWII) was approaching. In 1939 Stalin and Hitler signed a non-aggression pact between Germany and the Soviet Union. Stalin thought he could trust Hitler, who was by the way anti-Communist. Hitler was a Fascist, which is the authoritarianism style on the opposite side of the political spectrum. Unsurprisingly, the Nazi Germany broke the deal by striking the Soviet Union in June 1941. The Soviet Army was not ready to confront this invasion. Stalin became a recluse for several days in his office as Germany was occupying the at-the-time Soviet Republics of Ukraine and Belarus, causing the German artillery to surround Leningrad (or present-day St. Petersburg). As with any authoritarian who is surrounded by "Yes men/women," Stalin was very shortsighted in his planning process. All the purges that occurred in the 1930's also took away the talent and manpower from the Soviet Army and the government. Most people in power left were those loyal to Stalin, but not every one of those people were otherwise very bright. Yes man/woman tend to be one-dimensional.

Because the world had a common foe, being the Nazis, the Soviet Union became allied with the United States and Great Britain. This alliance forced the Nazis under Hitler and the Fascists under Mussolini to fight in two fronts. Even though the Soviet Army was not adequately manned by extremely skilled combatants, they still had large numbers compared to the rest of the military powers. Afterall the Soviet Union was the largest country in the world (although not the most populated).

The brutality of the Nazi regime incentivized the Soviets to fight tirelessly, and the Soviet Army was already gaining a trend of liberating Eastern European countries well before the allies were ready to take on the Germans during D-Day in the beaches of France. D-Day was the largest amphibious operation in history.

In fact, it was the Soviet Army who took over Berlin on May 2, 1945, just a few days after Hitler committed suicide in his bunker.

With that said, the Soviet Army did commit heinous crimes against humanity during these campaigns. And yes, that also included war crimes against German civilians. These were two authoritarian forces clashing, therefore they both committed dehumanizing horrors against each other. This was very contrary to the non-authoritarian – although imperfect – Western values. For example, citizens in the West did not get killed in the middle of the night if they spoke against the American President or the British Prime Minister.

Both sides of this equation were suspicious of each other from the start. American President Franklin D. Roosevelt and British Prime minister Winston Churchill were concerned about Stalin's brutality and tactics. For example, Stalin was onboard using tactics that would have millions of his own people die in the front lines. The Western allies were not onboard with the same school of thought. These disagreements just served to foment more suspicion against each other. Of course, millions of Soviet people both combatant and noncombatants died under Stalin's warfighting courses of action.

Stalin also wanted more control over liberated nations post WWII. Stalin was even willing to fight Japan after defeating Germany. By the later part of the war, United States President Roosevelt died, and President Harry S. Truman took his place. Great Brittan also replaced Churchill with Clement Attlee. He was going to be the Britain's main negotiator.

Both the British and Americans were very suspicious of Stalin intentions post WWII, especially as it pertained to Japan. The United

States dropped both atomic bombs in August 1945. This forced Japan to surrender, and in effect finished WWII before the Soviet Union had a chance to invade Japan. WWII was over, but his was only the beginning of a new conflict that would last several decades.

Stalin's paranoia against the West increased. And between 1945 and 1948 he expanded Communist regimes in many Eastern European countries to create a buffer between Russia proper and the rest of Western Europe. This rapid expansion of Communist power was interpreted by the West as the Soviet Union's attempt to engulf all Europe under Communist control.

In response to this, the North Atlantic Treaty Organization (NATO) was created. The aim was to stop any further Communist Soviet Influence.

In response, Stalin ordered an economic blockade of the city of Berlin in 1948 as an attempt to take full control of the city. The Allies supplied massive airlift support to Berlin in order to force Stalin to backtrack. This is one of the reasons why the Berlin Wall was erected. Germany at the time got divided between the Soviet Union and a few Western Countries. The Eastern Side of Germany was under Communist Control, while the other side was controlled by the West. Berlin itself was deep inside communist territory, that's why people could not just walk to the "end of the wall" and leave the country. The Berlin Wall was enclosing a small western "in-land-island" deep inside Soviet controlled territory. It was not until the fall of the Soviet Union that the wall was torn down and Germany once again became one.

The Soviet Union under Stalin aimed to keep the world blinded from what happened inside the Soviet borders. This is what was known as the "Iron Curtain." And this Iron Curtain lasted several decades after Stalin's death. But this closed-to-the- world reality also painted a utopian propagandistic scene for other Communist nations who emulated the Soviet Union as a feasible government method. But these regimes were also authoritarian and badly administrated.

Case in point, North Korea under Communist leader Kim Il Sung invaded South Korea under the pretense that the United States would not intervene. Well, they were wrong... the Korean war did occur. But that is another story, but it is worth mentioning that other authoritarians took notes from what they perceived Stalin as a political figure worth of emulation, even if this authorial model was flawed. And we have seen example after example in history to attest to this extreme form of governance inefficacy. Of course, people tend to believe that a flawed model is workable based on the propaganda that it is feed to them.

By the early 1950s Stalin's health continued to decline. A new purge of the Communist Party was ordered after an assassination plot was uncovered. However, Stalin died on March 5, 1953, among other things because he did not receive timely medical attention. Members of his inner circle in the party were afraid to even check on him, so when he had a hemorrhagic stroke, he was unable to call for help. That is what happens when a person is surrounded by "yes men/women."

Although Stalin died, his legacy superseded him to his day. The Soviet Union and Soviet Russia became a superpower during his tenure. Even the architecture Stalin favored was exuberant in contrast to the more simplistically utilitarian model that his successors adopted. Stalin killed as many as 20 million people (about the population of New York) due to famine, labor camps, collectivization, and of course summary executions. Stalin, although he attended and excelled in Seminar school, also outlawed religion while in power. Although the Soviet Union had to reverse that trend at some point in history due to some vast cultural traits across their many regions. But it is worth mentioning that although he imposed a secular regime by banning religion, this was more as a form of control because the party, his version of the party, became the deity of the land.

Stalin successors did reverse some of his policies, but the Soviet Union sedimented a lot of corruption from Stalin's times. And a lot of these trends became systematic, and normalized. Afterall, this standard was identical across the entire Soviet Union. Pair this with the fact that people were generally unable to explore outside Soviet borders, and this reality is what became normal to them. Yes, authoritarianism might feel normal to many if that is all they know. It is not unlike living in a household with an abusive parent. If a child is locked inside this environment, it will be very hard for them to understand what is wrong with it, or even rationalize if it is normal and acceptable. This normalization that started under Stalin is what set the stage for so many other authoritarians to copy, and worst it became part of many people's generational identity.

Some of the things that we do as part of our perception of the West against the East started when these atrocities occurred. Even though many people living today were not alive during those days, these cultural traits became normalized and passed through the generations. And yes, this bias occurs in both the East and the West to this day. That is why understanding propaganda, history, and enacting critical thinking paired with intellectual honesty is so important.

---— ***** ———

Francisco Franco | Spain
Born 04 DEC 1892 – Died 20 NOV 1975
Died of various health problems.

Regime in power from 1939 to 1975

Francisco Paulino Hermenegildo Teódulo Franco y Bahamonde or otherwise known as Francisco Franco Bahamonde was born in Spain 1892. He was also known as the "Generalísimo" which means "The Supreme General," and was also known as "Caudillo de España" which means "The leader of Spain." In either case Franco is another figure who sponsored countless deaths during his regime.

Franco achieved victory in the Spanish Civil War. From 1947 he had absolute power over Spain, and after his death the Spanish Monarchy was restored. That apparently was in line with Franco's wishes. A King in Spain could only be restored after he died. What a great guy! Huh? (Yes, that was sarcasm.)

Franco was aligned to extreme-right politics, which is very much akin to Hitler's Nazi party and Mussolini's Fascists. Franco was very much against Communists, who are on the opposite side of the authoritarian political spectrum (extreme-left). However, during WWII, Franco remained neutral – mostly because Spain had just endured several years of brutal Civil War. However, Franco did play both sides of the aisle by helping Jews to escape and provide some help to Germany during WWII.

Aside from all that, Franco was very much focused in giving Catholics a strong force within the law. Franco received help from Fascists when fighting the Spanish Civil war. As you can see there was already a strong religious bias in his character, and an obvious alignment with the church over to his side. Sadly, during WWII the Vatican was not exactly known for speaking against the crimes committed by right-wing-Catholic aligned dictators.

But Franco was not always this strong man Spain grew to fear. When he started his military career in 1907, he was not a very strong man at all. He wanted to join the Navy like his father before, but there were not enough quotas, so he ended up joining the Army. There are accounts that during military school they had to modify his rifle because it was too heavy for him. Despite this he rose thought ranks quite rapidly. At age 23, in 1916 he was the youngest officer of his kind in the Spanish Army.

Part of his cult of personality developed when he got wounded. The medics were not going to save him because he was as good as dead. He threatened the medic with a gun to treat him, they did... and to everyone's surprise he survived. Like many dictators who had a near death experience, this bolstered his confidence.

Franco was ruthless in many of the campaigns he took part in, but despite this he created a following of loyalist warriors in the front lines he served. These loyalists became key investments in future campaigns that helped Franco galvanize his power.

Particularly during the Spanish Civil War, his loyalists came to task from Africa, Italy, and Germany. Mussolini and Hitler helped Franco with planes and other heavy war machinery. Even though some of these war planes had Franco's insignia, they were flown by Italian and German troops. On September 21, 1936, Franco, who was in an independent command was given the title of Commander-in-Chief. One of his fellow revolutionaries Emilio Mola considered Franco unfit to serve, but Hitler who had a lot of skin in the game had preference for Franco. Of course, Hitler wanted compensation from these German efforts. Subsequently on October 1, 1936, Franco became the Head of State and *"Generalísimo"* of the Fascist Army in Spain. Mola died and this allowed Franco to raise into power, even though he had no connection to any political movement.

Life under Franco was brutal. The country was economically destroyed as result of the Civil War. There were thousands of summary executions, people in exile and large numbers of political prisoners. Most executions were against leftists, but he also targeted Spanish intelligentsia, moderate democratic left leaning people, atheists, and there were all kinds of martial courts and firing squads to kill people accused of treason.

Franco displayed the traits of an extreme-right strong man. For example, giving exponential power to the Catholic church and those with extreme-conservative views (yes, a person can become an extreme-conservative).

World War II (WWII) broke out in September 1939. On October 23, 1940, Hitler tried to have Franco enter the "Axis of Powers." Bottom line, Franco did not allow Spain to enter WWII. There is some divergency among historians about why. One account is that Francos demands were too steep for Hitler to agree, and others say that Spain was still torn up after the Civil War and Spain would have not been an effective ally at that time. My analysis would indicate a healthy mixture of both. Franco by that time had a lot of prestige as a good strategist, regardless of the help he got during the Civil War. Any setbacks would undermine his stance. In other words, my assessment is that this was more of a personality driven decision than a strategically altruistic one.

Even though Franco kind of played both sides of the aisle during WWII, when France collapsed in June 1940, Franco was more akin to be a non-combatant in support of these Axis-Powers. For instance, he let Germany put some ships in Spain, and some Spanish people volunteered, however unofficially, to fight alongside the Nazis. But contradictorily enough, Franco also allowed for safe passage to Jewish people fleeing France.

After WWII Spain was in isolation imposed by the United States and the United Kingdom. However, as the Cold War with the Soviet Union started, U.S. President Eisenhower brokered a deal with Franco known as the Pact of Madrid. This turned Spain who was impoverished after all these conflicts into a very wealthy nation. The Allies understood that Spain has a very strategic geographical location, therefore this created a situation that was favorable for Spain, regardless of the atrocities committed in the country. As a matter of fact, Spain became part of the United Nations in 1955. This extrinsic shift of world power dynamics allowed Spain to gain wealth into the 60's. This of course helped Franco remain power until his death.

However, there was also a very strong political and religious paradigm evolving as Franco normalized his ultra-conservative style of governing. He did not have a consistently aligned political vision, but rather he would derive his enforcing based on these right-wing and pro-Catholic ultra-religious interpretations. These were known as *nacionalsindicalismo and nacionalcatolicismo* respectively (National Syndicalism & National Catholicism).

Finally in 1969, Franco designated Prince Juan Carlos de Borbón the new tile of "Prince of Spain" to be his successor. Even though this prince had more liberal views, he enjoyed Franco's affection. And that makes sense because the prince's father should have technically been the next person in line to the throne. Finally, circa 1973 Franco stepped off from his title as *"Presidente de Gobierno,"* or Prime Minister. But like much other authoritarians in this list, he kept himself as the Commander in Chief of the Spanish Military Forces.

It was not until November 1975 when Franco finally passed away at the at the age of 82. Most conservative people thought that the new monarch would continue Francos ultra- conservative policies, but instead the now King of Spain restored democracy in Spain. The King even squashed an attempted coup in 1981. On a more curious note, there was a self- proclaimed "Pope Greofy XVII" of the right-wing Palmarian Catholic Church based primarily in Spain that canonized Franco as a saint. The actual Roman Catholic Church and the Vatican do not recognize Franco as a saint. But this goes to show the divergences and close links politics and religion can draw as they pertain to authoritarian figures.

———————— ***** ————————

Juan Perón | Argentina
Born 08 OCT 1895 – Died 01 JUL 1974
Died of a heart attack.

Regime in power from 1946 to 1974 (three different non-consecutive terms as he was in exile after second term)

Juan Domingo Perón was born in Argentina 1895. He was elected as Argentina's president three times. Two consecutive and one other time after he returned from exile. Perón was also a military officer.

Although he reformed Argentina's economy, it was at the cost of severe restrictions to civil liberties.

Perón, like many of the authoritarian leaders in this list, was not born into a rich family. At age 16 he entered military school to become an officer. He was tall, athletic, and very good at combat-type sports. In other words, the perfect stereotypical model of a military man for the time. His first post was as a military attaché in Chile, and he also went to Italy from 1938 to 1940 to observe Fascists doctrines.

In 1941 he returned to Argentina and organized a coup along with a secret group of officers known as *"Oficiales Unidos"* or "United Officers." The coup took place in 1943 and as a result he got the title of Secretary of Labor and Social Welfare. His influence grew and landed him the title of Secretary of War and later from 1944 through 1945 he served as the Vice President. As a miliary man he was also admired among the bulk of the military troops and the laborers in the country. In 1945 there was an attempt that included military members to repress Perón, but it failed.

Perón used mass media of the time, which was radio broadcast to reach several thousands of Argentinian citizens in order to establish himself as the Argentinian leader and was elected as such in 1946. Perón changed the law so he could be reelected in 1951, also he started imposing restrictions on civil liberties, touted industrialization and government intervention. His self- described government style was described as neither Communist nor Capitalist… it was however authoritarian. Fascist, in fact. One of Perón's greatest fortunes was his wife Eva Duarte, also known as "Evita" (yes, the same as the musical). She was charismatic and a huge advocate for his husband's policies. This helped Perón get the leverage to instill his policies. Even the less popular and repressive ones. Evita passed away of cancer in 1952.

Perón did make a lot of enemies during his time in office. He was also known for double standards, some that were in flagrant contrast with the Catholic Church. This caused many of his followers to retaliate against several churches leaving hundreds of civilians dead.

After his wife's death in the same year, he was removed from office and placed in exile. The people behind this removal were military leaders. Before he settled in Madrid, he first had to flee to Paraguay, which is across the border from Argentina. Despite the distance he still garnished support from his followers and returned to power in 1973 during a special election, 21 years after he went into exile. This time he instituted his new wife as the Vice President.

Much like his earlier terms he was positioned to the far right- wing politics, and regained alliances with labor groups. Perón died in 1974, and his wife Isabel became the president of Argentina until she too was removed in a coup of her own.

Perón, much like many other polarizing figures, had a legacy that transcended his own life. People in Argentina to this day either love or hate Perón. But most importantly, there are a lot of misconceptions and romanticism based on the cult of personality garnished by the appeal of an agreeable voice. In Perón's case, Evita. For goodness' sake, there is even a musical about them.

But their story is a lot more complex than the Broadway musical. For instance, Perón's last wife, who was also his Vice President was also detained for alleged human rights abuses while in power. These also are linked to abuses when her late husband was presiding over the country and in the two years after his death. The allegation accounts for over 15,000 political enemies' deaths. Though her defense was that she was ignorant of these occurrences, that does not negate the fact that these allegations occurred while they were in power.

There is a lot more about Perón's convoluted life, but I will move on by saying that his own double standards resonated with his followers. His platform served to misguide his country. Not everybody fell for it, that is why he was exiled. But he returned to power – which goes to show that constituents memories tend to be short-termed.

*****

Mao Zedong | China
Born 26 DEC 1893 – Died 09 SEP 1976
Died of a series of heart attacks.

Regime in power from 1943 to 1976

Mao Zedong (also known as Chairperson Mao) was born in Shaoshan, Hunan, Qing Dynasty, in present day People's Republic of China in 1893. Mao Tse-Tung (also known as Mao Zedong) held the position as the People's Republic of China chairperson from 1949 to 1959. Before the that time he led the Chinese Communist party from 1935 until dying of a heart attack in 1976. During his time in power, he improved some China relations around the world, such as opening relations with the United States, but he also had some catastrophic failures such as the "Great Leap Forward" and the "Cultural Revolution" which were responsible for some of the most horrific and profuse amounts deaths in the history of humanity.

Like many authoritarians in history, Mao was born during a precarious time. In Mao's case it was the 19th century, after the Qing Dynasty, China was in shambles. Mao was born on December 26, 1893, to a family of farmers who had worked the land for several generations. However, Mao's family life, although poor, was a lot more privileged than most people around that time. Mao's mother was a nurturing parent; while his father was a successful grain dealer who also happened to be very authoritarian. Mao received some education when he was a child, but by age 13 he was sent to work the fields full time. During this period, he grew his frustrations and ambitions. He ultimately became a primordial Marxist theorist in China. These were catalysts for him to follow the life of a military man and become the head of state after enacting China's Cultural Revolution.

But well before all that when he was only 14 years old, Mao's father arranged a marriage for his son. Mao did not accept this marriage and left home age 17. By 1911 Mao joined the Xinhua Revolution against the monarch. He became part of the Revolutionary Army and the Kuomintang, which was the Nationalist Party. These forces ousted the monarchy in 1912 resulting in the founding of the Republic of China. Mao was very happy about political and cultural changes occurring in China after the monarchy fell.

As time moved on, Mao had ups and downs without significant success nor tribulations. But when he was working as librarian assistant at the Beijing University, he heard about the successes of the Russian Revolution which led to the establishment of the Soviet Union. This ideology had a great impact on Mao, and in 1921 he became one of the first members of the Chinese Communist Party.

Mao rose thorough the party's ranks. By this time his political views have morphed into a Leninist ideology; particularly those that related to famers as the key to establishing communism throughout Asia.

When Sun Yat-sen, who was the Chinese President died in March 1925, his successor Chiang Kai-shek became the chairman. However, this new leader was traditionalist and conservative – in other words was he swaying towards the right-wing more than the left-wing vision of the party. By April 1927 the new chairperson started a violent killing and imprisonment of Communists in China. Mao got the support of peasants to create an army to try to defeat the incumbent Kuomintang, but it failed. The survivors of this army fled to the Jiangxi mountains. It was here where Mao was instrumental in establishing the Soviet Republic of China and became the chairperson of this small republic. These new fighters engaged in guerrilla style fighting. Also, their tactics consisted of torture and killing of any dissidents to their new party's ideology.

In October 1942 Chiang Kai-shek in responded with a massive campaign intended to eradicate Communist influence. This led to what is known as the "Long March" when 100,000 Communists and their families fled through the mountains and the swamplands. It is estimated that only 30% of them survived this 8,000-mile journey. Mao was a prolific orator who inspired people to volunteer and pledge their faith towards him as the top Communist leader. However, around the same time in July 1937 as the Japanese Imperial Army invaded China, this forced Chiang Kai-shek to negotiate a truce with the Communists as he needed support. Mao then appointed himself the leader of the military along with allied forces to fight and defeat the Japanese in 1945. Remember, around this time the world was embroiled in World War II (WWII).

By this time Mao has postured himself to take control of China. The Western Allies wanted to set up a coalition government, but instead China entered a horrific civil war. On October 1, 1949, Mao announced the establishment of the People's Republic of China in Tiananmen Square, Beijing. Chiang Kai-shek along with his followers fled to the land of Taiwan to form the Republic of China.

As Mao took control, he started a series of reforms in China. Some were good such as literacy, education raising the status of women and health care which of course improved life expectancy in the country. A lot of the other policies were terrible, and we will talk about that. If people were not onboard with his policies he would use coercion, terror, or violence in order to impose his will.

Mao was not very well received in the cities, and this caused him to try to figure out what he could do better. When he received poignant criticism to his policies, Mao retaliated by brutally eliminating any dissent. If a Chinese person was labeled as right-winger (rightist), they would be imprisoned and punished.

Mao was fearful that the people in the cities would challenge his grab on control, therefore he established harsher doctrines to assert his authority. This led to the "Great Leap Forward in January 1958. His plan was to improve agricultural and industrial production – a similar model used in the *Stalin*-led Soviet Union (which was not actually successful either, by the way). The premise was to have large shared agricultural communes, which was to assign each family a small share of the profits and they had to work a small plot of land. This followed an idealistic idea used by the Soviets, but it was not sustainable in practice. In paper they thought they could accelerate in a few years what would take centuries to accomplish. Of course, this did not work as they intended.

Mao did not account for factors that could derail the plan such as environmental factors that destroyed the harvests. Even though it had a positive start, this disastrous program led to the worst famine in the history of the world accounting for 40 million people (about twice the population of New York) dying of starvation from 1959 to 1961. Essentially killing entire villages. And to add insult to injury the industry reports were not accurate. Which is a euphemism to say that industrial production was misleading at best. It was also a gigantic failure. Mao was a good strategist when it came to organize revolutions, but he was lousy at administrating this perceived utopia he created. Much like in the Soviet Union, the truth about this disaster was hidden to the world <u>and</u> to the rest of the nation. It is being said that even Mao was unaware of this reality and only some very high-level Communist Party leaders knew about these failures that lead to countless deaths.

Because of this famine, Mao was pushed however quietly to the side in 1962 as his rivals took the reins of the country. After 25 years Mao was not the center of China's leadership. However, there was a change coming. Lin Biao, who was a strong Mao supporter created a little handbook known as the "Little Red Book" which contained several quotes from Mao. Copies of this little red book were distributed all over China.

Fast forward to 1966, Mao made a gigantic political return when he launched the "Cultural Revolution". In order to prove his vitality Mao, now 73 years old, swam in the river for several minutes to show that he was fit and energetic. This time he targeted the younger men. The message was "Look, I am Back!" – a highly choreographed marketing (propaganda) campaign aimed at the younger generations. Mao figured correctly that much of the younger people will not recall or even know about his failures on the Great Leap Forward – which led to the worst famine in the history of the world. He was correct, people tend to have very short memories, or lack historical understanding.

As China was trying to restore capitalist principles, Mao used this as a manufactured crisis to gain control and claimed that he was the only one who could solve this problem. This is a common tactic used by authoritarians. Create buzz for a problem that does not really exist, appoint somebody or something as the foe, and rally support to fight this imaginary problem or foe. And if it is not imaginary, just pretend that nobody else on the entire planet is qualified to handle this "imponent" problem or foe.

This prompted his young followers to form the Red Guard, and this started yet another purge of people who were against Mao's ideology. Mao then closed schools and sent the young intellectuals living in the cities to the countryside to perform hard manual labor in order to "re-educate them." Mao also destroyed much of China's cultural heritage and traditions. This gave Mao a way to expand his cult of personality by purging dissenting cultural traits in the country.

When 1972 came around then United States President Nixon opened relations with China. This was a gesture to ease tensions between both countries and made China a prominent player on the world stage. By this time Mao's health was in severe decline and he was becoming less coherent in his declarations and doctrines.

On September 9, 1976, at the age of 82, Mao passed away due to complications related to Parkinson's disease resulting in heart failure. Though he has a proficient political and military figure, as far as rallying support from his followers, he also left behind some of the worst atrocities against humanity, which included his own people. His authoritarian style caused the death of millions. His opposition for being open to any dissenting opinions and doctrines made it harder for Chinese people to speak their mind. Some of the geopolitical events that occurred during his tenure also opened the way to posture China as a global leader, such as the opening relations with the United States in the early 70's. Although he is still a polarizing figure, it is worth recognizing that his policies for better or worse transcended his own existence, and those young minds he was able to convince to commit atrocities on his behalf are still alive today. Think about this last part for a moment.

---***** ---

Vladimir Lenin | Soviet Union
Born 22 APR 1870 – Died 21 JAN 1924
Died of atherosclerosis.

Regime in power from 1917 to 1924

Vladimir Ilyich Ulyanov was born in the Russian Empire, present day Russia 1883. Few political figures are as well recognized as Vladimir Lenin. Even if you do not know much about him, you are surely to have seen his likeness in a statue or any other Soviet paraphernalia. Lenin founded the Russian Communist Party and was the leader the of the Bolshevik Revolution which led to him to create and become the trailblazer of the Soviet State.

Like many authoritarians Lenin was born with a different name. Vladimir Ilich Ulyanov was born in Simbirsk, Russia on April 22, 1870. This city was later renamed Ulyanovsk in his honor in 1901. He changed his last name to Lenin when he was working with the underground party. Despite being coined a champion of the less fortunate, Lenin came from a highly cultured and educated family. They instilled education and access to literature, and Lenin even became very proficient in Latin and Greek.

His destiny was shaped when his father was threatened with an early retirement because the government was nervous about their influence on Russian society. Another decisive blow to his life was when Lenin's older brother was arrested and executed in 1887 for being part of a group that was planning to assassinate Emperor (Tsar) Alexander III. By this time Lenin's father was dead, making him the head of the household and looking after the rest of his family.

The entire family was politically active in the sense they opposed the current political regime and did partake in revolutionary activities in one way or the other. For example, the same year his brother was killed, Lenin as expelled from the university for participating in a politically charged student demonstration. He was exiled to live with his grandparents for this cause, his grandfather was also under suspicion of similar opposing political activities. During this time Lenin became an avid reader of radicalized literature, and studied the writings for German's philosopher Karl Marx who wrote Das Kapital. This defined Lenin and in 1889 he became a Marxist.

Lenin received his law degree in 1892 and was in charge of representing mainly Russian peasants. The existing social class disparity and congruent biases in the law served to reaffirm his Marxists views. Lenin continued to network with other Marxists which increased his prominence in these activities.

Subsequently, Lenin founded the Russian Communist Party, and in 1917 he led the Bolshevik Revolution. His influence created what is known as Marxism-Leninism which expanded his Communist interpretations around the world, placing Lenin as the most influential revolutionary leader since Marx. This influence allowed him to become the first leader of the Union of Soviet Socialist Republics (USSR), also known as the Soviet Union.

Still, things were not as simple leading to this goal. In December 1895, Lenin among many other Marxist were arrested and exiled. Lenin ended up in Siberia, but that did not stop him. Lenin then co-founded a newspaper to unify Marxists in Russia and Europe. The publication "Iskra," would assert that if they garnished enough revolutionaries support, they would overturn Russia.

As has been in many other times in history, extrinsic events played a key role in the placement of an authoritarian figure. In this case, Russia went to war with Japan in 1904. This of course badly damaged the Russian's economy, and the response from society was a loud dissent with the incumbent political structure, opening the floodgates for change. This escalated, and on January 9, 1905, an unarmed group of workers went to the palace to speak with Emperor Nicholas II. The monarch's security shot the group, killing and wounding hundreds of them. This abuse of power and brutality of course became a catalyst for the Revolution.

The monarchy tried to ease the tensions by creating something known as the Duma, which was an elected legislative assembly. Lenin and his comrades disagreed with this and argued that Russia should be led by the proletariat, otherwise known as the country's workers.

Lenin's vision was to rally the people to support a one-man dictatorship – which was himself, of course. And this man had ability to empower all workers. However, this was also managed by a small group hand-picked by Lenin, the Bolsheviks, who enjoyed only a very narrow majority.

As World War I (WWI) raged, Lenin was pushed into exile once again. This time he was in in Switzerland and asserted that war is always the result of capitalism around the world. Hence, Soviets demonized capitalism. The conditions for Lenin became best when in 1917 the inequality in Russia finally reached the point that overthrew the Tsars. Lenin returned to Russia and denounced the provisional government which was assembled by the Bourgeois liberal parties. The same type of party the monarch used as concessions years back, and the same type of group Lenin distrusted. Lenin of course then called for a rule of soldiers, peasants, and workers. In essence, the Soviet Union.

The October Revolution occurred at the end of the year 1917. This three-year civil war was brutal. Tsar supporters and the monarch's military fought bitterly to try to overthrow Lenin's Soviet forces, or what was known as Lenin's Red Regime. There were even WWI

Allies who got involved in some shape or form by supplying the group with money and troops.

Lenin launched what came to be known as the "Red Terror," where Lenin ruthlessly cut the opposition in the Russian civilian population. Lenin narrowly escaped assassination in August 1918, even though he was never fully recovered from the bullet impacts that he received.

Lenin finally came to power, but his victory was relative. Poverty and famine existed very much during his tenure. His opposition and even his supporters who helped him reach power would instigate revolts and strikes in the cities and the countryside. By distancing themselves from the capitalist European model, the Soviet Union kept getting more and more isolated from the rest of the world. However, Lenin would convince himself and his supporters that this would also help them stay away from other wars, and that everybody in the country would be considered equals.

However idealistic his model was, it was not sustainable. Lenin then introduced an economic policy that would allow the workers to sell their grain in the open market in an attempt to calm down the population.

Lenin's health continued to deteriorate, and during May and later in December 1922 he suffered strokes. Lenin started the inevitable thought process of who would govern the USSR if he passed away. He realized that his party and government had not been steadfast to his original revolutionary goals. By this time Lenin was disappointed that Joseph Stalin who was the General Secretary of the Communist party had been able to amass a lot of power. This was concerning to Lenin, because it was him who was a catalyst to help position Stalin into such a desirable position at the Soviet party.

Lenin's health took a turn for the worse on March 10, 1923. His next stroke took away Lenin ability to speak and therefore govern. Lenin died on January 21, 1924, his body was embalmed and placed in a mausoleum in Moscow. Lenin's remains are still in Red Square to this day. As the architect of the Soviet Union, he is still revered by many people who lived in Soviet times. Under the Russian Orthodox church, there are even Icons devoted to him. Yes, as a saint. That is even though he brutally killed thousands upon thousands of people who disagreed with his political views.

---***** ---

Adolf Hitler | Germany
Born 20 APR 1889 – Died 30 APR 1945
Died by suicide.

Regime in power from 1933 to 1945

Adolf Hitler was born in Austria 1889. Likely know as one of the evilest people in human history, Hitler was so polarizing that even his relatives changed their last name as to leave no trace of his horrors. Unfortunately, there are still many who fully support the atrocities he advocated for while he was alive. Hitler was the leader of Nazi Germany; this was an extreme far-right movement with a Fascist-like agenda. He led the world into World War II, and was responsible for more than 11 million deaths, to include the extermination of six million Jews.

Hitler's father was emotionally punitive, and quite disapproving of Hitler's interest in fine arts as a career. Turns out Hitler never did become a very successful artist. But there was another emotional turning point in Hitler's early life. In 1900 his brother Edmund died, causing this young boy to become withdrawn and disengaged with those around him. Despite this, from an early age he showed interest in German nationalism and rejection of what was known as Austria-Hungary. By the way, Hitler was born in Austria. In either case this nationalism became a source of motivation for young Hitler.

Hitler's father died suddenly in 1903, and a few years later, in 1907 his mother also died. He moved to Vienna and applied to the Academy of Fine arts but was rejected, twice. He made a meager living as watercolor painter. As he was struggling and spending his nights in homeless shelters, he started cultivating anti-Semitism during his personally difficult times. This account has been subject to debate according to historians, but I can see how there is a plausibility that this dire strain would have misguided him to find a scape goat onto anybody who in his view might have seem to enjoy a much stronger family unit and success than he did at that time.

Hitler moved to Munich, Germany in 1913. This is the circa the time when World War I (WWI) started. He applied and was accepted to serve in the German army in 1914, even though he was an Austrian citizen. Hitler did not spend too much time in the front lines, but he did take part in several important battles. There is even an account of a near death experience, and that gave him an *epiphany* that he had a higher purpose. For his participation in WWI, he was awarded the Iron Cross First Class and the Black Wound Badge. These WWI events were also instrumental in enticing the masses as he rose to power.

Hitler returned to Munich after WWI, where he continued to work for the German military as an intelligence officer. He was directed to monitor the German Worker's Party (DAP). However, he started to be enticed by their doctrines and this was another catalyst where he sedimented many of his anti-Semitic, nationalist, and anti-Marxist views. Hitler was very critical of the Treaty of Versailles. In his view this degraded Germany by accepting responsibility for starting WWI. Even though Hitler was supposed to spy on the DAP he become one of them in September 1919.

The DAP changed its name to the Nationalsozialistische Deutsche Arbeiterpartei (NSDAP) commonly known Nazi. Hitler was so enamored with this organization that he even designed the Nazi party banner by appropriating the swastika and placing it in a white circle on a red background. This emblem will be later synonymous with some of the most horrific crimes against humanity in the history of the world. Hitler's notorious speeches and the way he was able to resonate with people who were ready for extremism and antisemitism led him to become the chairperson of the Nazi party.

One of the places where Hitler grew his audience was on the beer halls. The audiences gained regulars and increased in numbers. On November 8, 1923, Hitler declared the formation of a new government via a national revolution. This was known as the Beer Hall Pustch. Hitler declared his so-called revolution and was later arrested for treason and sentenced to nine months in prison. A very lenient sentence if you consider that later the Nazis dehumanized and killed people for a lot less.

While in prison Hitler dictated his autobiographical manifesto called *"Mein Kampf,"* which translates to "My Struggle." His deputy was Rudolf Hess. Another notorious Nazi who was later an acolyte in perpetrating heinous crimes against humanity. He wrote two volumes, the first published in 1925 and the second in 1927. These books were full of propaganda, false statements, and described his plan to transform Germany into a supreme race country. These vile publications were translated into 11 languages and sold an excess of five million copies.

In the first volume he goes on a rampage sharing his racist pro-Aryan and anti-Semitic views, as well as his misguided assertion of betrayal after WWI. He goes onto call for revenge against other countries, particularly France.

His second volume pertained to his plan to gain and maintain power. When these volumes are read pragmatically you would realize how poorly written they are. It is the ramblings of a madman, and I am not just talking about the grammatical errors, but also the logical fallacies throughout this entire tirade. However, those logical shortcomings did not matter in the great scheme of things as Hitler hit his mark by capitalizing on the biases of Germans who felt disenfranchised after WWI. His divisive rhetoric, however illogical, was able to convince thousands of people with propensity to extremism to become receptive to this message of hate.

And Hitler found himself in a very favorable position to spread this misinformation. At the time, Germany was also victim of the Great Depression, and there were millions of Germans unemployed. Hitler decided to run for the presidency in 1932 against Paul Von Hindenburg. Hitler was the runner up the two times he tried, but he was able to get more than 36% of the votes. This gave Hitler legitimacy in German politics. Hitler was then appointed as Chancellor, even though Hindenburg was not fully onboard with this decision. However, in his view he thought this would help his cause as a way of providing political balance. Now, we all realize that this was not a good decision.

As chancellor, Hitler ramped up detentions without trial and the suspension of German people's rights. To this end, he used the Reichstag Fire Decree as a pretext in the aftermath of a suspicious fire at the German's parliament. He also introduced the Enabling Act after some clever politics in order to legalize deviations to the constitution that were favorable to him and his cabinet. These were supposed to be "temporary" for only four years. Of course, we know how *that* ended up. Hitler used this chancellor position to function as a dictator. He proclaimed himself as Führer, which translates as "leader." With this power grab, he took control over all branches of government.

Soon after Hitler and his cronies started to suppress and dismantle all political opposition in the country. On July 14, 1933, the Nazi party was the only legal political party in the country, and in 1934 Germany withdrew from the League of Nations. Hitler also punished military opposition. For example, starting on June 30 until July 2, 1934, Hitler conducted a series of assassinations in what it is known as the Night of the Long Knives. These assassinations occurred all over the country. People were hunted down and murdered.

A day before Hindenburg passed away in 1934, Hitler's cabinet have legally abolished the office of the president and passing all powers to the chancellor. Aside from giving power over all of government, he was also the supreme commander of the German Armed Forces. But his power grab was already in overdrive well before that time. As early as 1933 Hitler had legalized restrictions and exclusions of Jews in German society, and of course this led to the prosecution of Jewish people.

Hitler fanatism was even harsh on himself, he abstained from drinking alcohol or eating meat. This was also part of his campaign for a superior Aryan race, in which advocated Aryans from keeping their bodies free of toxic substances such as smoking. But this fanatism was also implemented to disenfranchise and dehumanize Jewish people and their businesses from every aspect of life. This boycott continued to increase, not only by making Jewish people's life more difficult, but to prolong their suffering. In other words, the systematic destruction of their lives and any opportunity for them to exist. He even banned Jewish people from performing in film or in the theater.

By 1935 Hitler expanded the definition of "Jew" in order to maximize this agenda of hate. Even if the person labeled Jew was not technically Jewish or did not practice a Jewish religion. Arbitrarily under his view, a person would be labeled "Jew" if three out of four grandparents were Jewish.

Book burnings also became a thing. Like many extremists, Hitler aimed to destroy any knowledge that could be dissention to his misguided views. This of course was labeled as "Actions Against the Un-German Sprit." Students burned well over 25,000 books. Of course, this hate was not limited only against Jewish people. In fact, this eventually extended to all "non- Aryans." The "Law for the Protection of German Blood and German Honor" would deny German citizenship to any person who did not qualify as Aryan himself or herself. Which incidentally, Hitler himself did not fully qualify under his own insane metric.

The world was taking notice, but in 1936 Germany hosted the Winter and Summer Olympic Games in order to improve tourism and quelch criticism on the world stage. The sad truth is that it was not only Germany who was insanely racist back in those decades, there were plenty of very racist's countries around the world too. The Nazis merely were able to enact insane laws by exploiting the biases of a population who was already susceptible to extremism. In fact, right after the Olympics the prosecutions intensified, and it only got worse and worse for any "non-Aryan" – especially Jewish people. This also started a trend of having them mark their passports and their clothing with symbols (such as the Star of David) that will make obvious their Jewish heritage. This of course was a tactic to make it easier for the Nazis to discriminate and enact violence against them. Destruction of synagogues and ransacking of Jewish homes were all too common, and deaths by murder continued to ramp up.

There is something called *Kristallnacht*, which translates to the "Night of Crystal" or the "Night of Broken Glass," where about 30,000 Jewish men were arrested and sent to concentration camps. Hitler also prosecuted people with disabilities and homosexuals. Even children were not spared, especially those with disabilities were subject of eugenic and euthanasian practices to include sadistic medical experiments. Much like Jewish people, people who were attracted to their same sex were forced to wear a symbol, in this case it was a pink triangle. The Nazis believed that homosexuality was a disease, yet that was also treated as a crime. It goes without saying but let us emphasize that homosexuality is not a disease nor is it criminal. Nazis were just as misinformed about this as about everything else they perpetrated against humankind.

Between 1939 to 1945 which is the official entirety of World War II (WWII), the Nazis and their cronies were responsible for six-million (or two-thirds) of the Jewish people killed in Europe. But they also killed many other human beings accounting for more than 11-million noncombatant deaths. Add to this figure the millions of military casualties around the world and the number becomes incalculable.

Hitler was the catalyst for some of the most deprived creativity from his followers. When they Nazis were killing people all over Europe, they found they were not efficient enough. Dealing with the bodies or even spending bullets was apparently a nuisance for Hitler's depraved followers. There were people under him finding ways to exterminate as many people as possible and make it easier on those killing them. This is what is known as Hitler's "Final Solution," or what is commonly known as the Holocaust. This genocidal act is unfortunately denied from even occurring according to some deluded people even to this day.

These deaths and mass executions took place in many places throughout the occupied territories. Some of those include Auschwitz-Birkenau, Treblinka, Dachau, Bergen-Belsen, and many others. These concentration camps were also execution camps. These places also held Communists, Jehovah Witnesses, trade unionists, Poles, people with disabilities, etc., aside from Jewish people. These prisoners were forced to perform excruciating manual labor. Their living conditions were squalid. People were starved, tortured, and endured many other dehumanizing brutalities such as human medical experimentation. Hitler did not speak publicly about these concentration camps or their crimes. However, Germans documented very thoroughly their crimes both in film and very detailed paper records. Why you think is that? Because they thought their crimes were considered morally acceptable and justified by those who perpetrated said crimes.

I am going to leave it at this for now. Unfortunately, there is a lot to more to discuss about Hitler, and that is why you can always find countless books and documentaries about him, his regime of terror, and all the horrific derivatives from his misguided rhetoric. But for the purpose of this book, I really want you to notice the indicators that brought him into power. Pay special attention to the geopolitical situation during those years, and how the minds of the general populace were vulnerable to exploitation. Hitler was not actually a very smart man, and he got more and more reckless as the war continued. He was just able to convince a lot of other people about a false narrative that he was very much likely convinced about himself. He was persuasive, and paradoxically enough, fortunately he was not bright. He was cunning, but not in-fact smart. Why do I keep emphasizing this?

As WWII continued, Hitler surrounded himself by "yes man and women." Some of his ideas were terrible, and his strategic calculations were atrocious. However, he would not listen to his senior officers. He often overruled their recommendations on a whim. This caused the Nazis a lot of loses, even though they started quite strong. But as we all know the allied powers which included the United States, Great Britain and the Soviet Union were able to surround him and brought his regime to an end. And although the United States wanted to remain neutral, when the Japanese attacked Pearl Harbor on December 7, 1941, the United States entered the war. The Japanese of course were allied with Germany during WWII.

Another huge strategic mistake took place on June 22, 1941, when Hitler violated the non-aggression pact with the Soviet Union. Now Hitler had enemies on both fronts. And of course, eventually the allied forces surrounded him after defeating Mussolini on the southern flank. By early 1945 Hitler already knew he was fighting a losing war. Hitler committed suicide on April 30, 1945, along with his one-day wife Eva Braun inside his underground bunker in Berlin. The day before, Hitler heard about Mussolini's death, and he feared that if captured he would suffer a similar fate. Mussolini was mercilessly and brutally executed, and his body was put on display.

Hitler and Braun took cyanide poison and then he shot himself in the head. Hitler was 56 at the time of suicide. Their remains were doused with gasoline and burned. His cause of death was proven years after when the remains were exuded and examined.

The Soviet military took Berlin on May 2, 1945, and on May 7, 1945, Germany surrenders unconditionally. Although Hitler avoided multiple assassination attempts by dumb luck, his destiny was marked by the crimes he perpetrated against humanity. He, like any other authoritarian realized that his power was not unlimited. Even though the Nazis were able to convince many followers to commit atrocities in their behalf, they never had a clear vision for what they were doing. They were always chasing a falsehood that came across disconnected in the ramblings of a frustrated and conflicted mad man.

The problem is that this mad man enjoyed an immense following. Some of his following extend to this day. However, even the Neo-Nazis are still confused about the false reality he tried to portray. Hitler's doctrine has so many gigantic logical plot holes that you can fly planes through them. And that makes sense, because his assertions were never based on fact. They were based on conjecture. And that is another reason that makes this rhetoric extremely dangerous. Some people do not care about facts, and will prefer to immerse themselves into a falsehood, rather than being correct. For the record, that is not the right way to live. Accepting falsehoods willingly, knowing very well that they are false is in fact stupid.

———————— ***** ————————

Muammar Gaddafi | Libya
Born 1942 – Died 20 OCT 2011
Died of gunshot wound.

Regime in power from 1969 – to 2011

Muammar Muhammad Abu Minyar al-Gaddafi was born in Libya 1942. He was also known as Muammar al-Qaddafi or simply as "Qaddafi." He took power of the Libyan government via a military coup in 1969. Qaddafi became an authoritarian dictator and remained in power for just a little over four decades until his regime was overthrown in 2011.

Qaddafi was born on June 7, 1942. He was raised in a Bedouin tent in the Libyan desert. He was part of the al-Qadhafah tribe. Libya was at the time an Italian colony until it gained independence in 1951. Qaddafi from a young age was fascinated with the he Arab Nationalist Movement. Around this point in time Libya gained independence and was placed under the control of King Idris. The King was a Western ally. Qaddafi discontent against the King grew as time went by. Qaddafi started his military career in 1961 at the military college in Benghazi. His military training also included a few months in the United Kingdom. As a charismatic and talented military man, Qaddafi rose through the ranks of the Libyan military with relative ease.

Qaddafi became part of a group of young military officers who were preparing a coup against King Idris. Qaddafi became one of the main leaders for this group. The coup took place on September 1, 1969, while the King was receiving medical treatment in Turkey. The 27 years-old Qaddafi was named Commander in Chief of the Armed Forces and the Chairperson of the Revolutionary Command Council which was now in charge of Libya. This position made him the de facto leader for the entire country.

It did not take long for this young ruler to enact his authoritarian agenda. His first step was the shutting down of the American and British military bases in the country. He also commanded that any foreign oil companies operating in Libya had to share a larger part of the profits. He also instituted the use of the Islamic calendar, as well as other Islamic rules such as turning Libya into a dry country by prohibiting the sale of alcohol.

In 1969 Qaddafi made it not only unlawful but criminal to disagree with him. This was a reactionary tactic after a failed coup occurred involving his fellow officers at the end of that year. As 1970 rolled in, Qaddafi expelled any Italian and Jewish people who were still living in the country. This was part of his so called "anti-Western imperialism" rule, but of course it was also about his very vocal opposition to Zionism. As his power grab increased his circle of trusted people shrank. He became more and more paranoid and even sent his operatives to other countries in order to kill any Libyan expats, especially those in exile. This of course also distanced Libya from the West, and it aligned his regime closer with Africa and the Middle East. It became common place for Libya the part of military conflicts in Africa, which included civil wars.

As the 70's continued he published his political philosophy in what was known as the "Green Book." This was a three-volume propaganda publication where he makes himself the central figure and boasts of being the only person who can fix any problem that pertains to the population. The publication went on to describe his interpretation in regards with the problems with capitalism, rhetoric against liberal views, promotion of shared ownership and other gripes he had. This propaganda tool was supposed to prove that equality existed among the Libyan population. Of course, this was not true at all, because the wealth inequality grew exponentially as him and his closest cronies benefited from the Libyan oil revenue. And of course, anybody who dissented was murdered, even if they fled the country. Every position of power was only given to Qaddafi, his family and all his closest "yes man/women" allies. Yes, I repeated this for a reason.

The excess continued to grow and got out of control. Qaddafi became extremely eccentric, which made his regime increasingly bizarre on top of being exceedingly oppressive. He was nicknamed "the mad dog of the Middle East. For example, he had an all-female bodyguard personal security detail who were required to wear heels. His outfits looked like very elaborate costumes and had his people erect a tent anytime he was visiting abroad. This eccentricity somehow served to skew the perception of the atrocities and the many crimes that occurred under his regime.

Libyans themselves hated this despotic dictator, but they were living under his heel. The international community was not welcoming of him either, or very soon gained notoriety among world leaders. This was especially true because Libya financed many terrorist groups, especially those who were conducting anti-Western operations. This of course caused several diplomatic breakdowns with several countries around the world. Some of these acts of terrorism include but are not limited to the 1986 West Berlin discotheque (dance club). Of course, these were Cold War era times, and that was when the infamous Berlin Wall still existed, and Berlin was divided between East and West. East Berlin was under Communist rule. Later in 1988, a plane bombing killed 259 people near Lockerbie Scotland. In 1989 another plane bombing, this time in France killed all 170 passengers onboard.

Although Qaddafi and the west exchanged firepower several times during these decades, things began to take a turn in the 90's. By this time the Soviet Union had fallen, and there was a growing number of Islamist who opposed Qaddafi's regime. This prompted Qaddafi to share names of people responsible from some of the atrocities under his watch to American and British intelligence agencies. Even Nelson Mandela from Africa was able to convince Qaddafi to share some of that information. This worked in Qaddafi's favor as the relations with the West improved in many aspects. Though Qaddafi was still an authoritarian.

Many people around the world realized the obvious, this friendship of convenience with Qaddafi was transactional in nature. Especially because it had links to oil and secondary businesses. Qaddafi even welcomed Western capitalists and world leaders. Even Italian Prime Minister Silvio Berlusconi became one of his closest friends. And it is worth remembering that just a few decades before Qaddafi expelled every Italian from Libya. Even Qaddafi's son started to mingle with London's high society. This was a very stark change and for many observers quite a bizarre transformation in the geopolitical realm indeed.

The trend continued when in 2001 the United Nations eased sanctions on Libya and any oil companies working in connection with this country. Of course, this made Qaddafi's fortune and personal income grow exponentially. However, the disparity between the regime and the rest of the population became even more contrasting. This was a period of relative comfort for Qaddafi, and even his eccentricity was no longer as prominent on the world stage. It simply got normalized. Things were about to change dramatically when the Arab Spring arrived. His four decades in power ended in less than one year.

In January 2011 Tunisians deposed their very own dictator Zine al-Albidine Ben Ali. This started what is historically known as the Arab Spring. February of the same year Egypt removed Hosni Mubarak, and this embolden other Arab countries to follow suit. This was also true for Libya and more demonstrations started to percolate throughout the country. Qaddafi escalated the situation by enacting violence against the protestors. This even included mercenaries, police and helicopters bombing the protestors from the air. The citizens of Libya had enough and were determined to oust their despotic dictator.

As expected, Qaddafi used his platform on state television to ramble about all kinds of falsehoods and to rally support from his loyalists around the country. He went on to label any dissenting person as traitors, al-Qaeda terrorists, drug addicts, and even blamed these very Libyans citizens of being foreign antagonists. By the end of February 2011, the rebels have prevailed over most of the country and created what was known as the National Transitional Council (NTC).

In April, the North Atlantic Treaty Organization (NATO) had killed one of Qaddafi's sons, and by late August Tripoli fell. But still, this was only a symbolic conclusion to Qaddafi's regime. However, even as early as June 2011 there were warrants issued for Qaddafi's arrest issued by the International Criminal Court for crimes against humanity. By July more than 30 countries had recognized the NTC as the official government in Libya. Nobody could find Qaddafi during this entire time. Finally on October 20, 2011, it was officially announced that Qaddafi was killed near his hometown of Sirte. There is video that shows Qaddafi's bloodied body being dragged by the opposition who was largely comprised of his own citizens. Qaddafi, like many despotic leaders, found himself alone and afraid when the tables were turned on him.

Though I do not condone inhumane treatment against any human being, most of the people who charged against Qaddafi had suffered under his heel. Also, Qaddafi was responsible for countless deaths and lived in impunity until that moment. All of Qaddafi's "yes men and women" ultimately left his side when it was proven to them that the power of his brutal regime came to an end.

*****

Saddam Hussein | Iraq
Born 28 APR 1937 – Died 30 DEC 2006
Died of execution by hanging.

Regime in power from 1979 to 2003

Saddam Hussein Abd al-Majid al-Tikriti was born in Iraq in 1937. For over two decades Saddam Hussein was the president of Iraq, and the person in charge of the country during military conflicts against Iran, Kuwait, and the United States. But before that Saddam Hussein's like many other authoritarians around the world, also had a very traumatic childhood. His father was a shepherd, but he disappeared several months before Saddam Hussein was born. His mother was very depressed because also her oldest son died. When Saddam Hussein was only three years old, he was sent to live with his uncle Khairallah Talfah. Eventually he returned to his hometown to live with his mother, but ended up fleeing because his stepfather was abusive to him. As Saddam Hussein settled back in Bagdad with his uncle, he was influenced by this man's Arab Nationalist politics and devotion to the Sunni Muslim interpretation of Islam. This helped forge Saddam Hussein's ideology from a young age.

When Saddam Hussein turned 20, he joined the Ba'ath Party whose purpose was to unite Arab states in the Middle East. On October 7, 1959, Saddam Hussein and others in this group attempted to kill Abd al-Karim Quasim, who was Iraq's president at the time. Quasim, even though he was shot several times survived. In this firefight Saddam Hussein got shot in the leg, but he managed to escape to Syria. Most others in the group were caught and executed.

Eventually Quasim's government ended in 1963 when he was ousted in what its known as the "Ramadan Revolution." When Saddam Hussein returned to Iraq, he was arrested for his involvement in the Ba'ath party a few years back. Even though he was in prison, he continued to be involved in politics. In 1966 he was appointed as the Deputy Secretary of the Regional Command. Subsequently he managed to escape from prison and continued to grow his political influence.

Saddam Hussein took part in the successful Ba'athist coup in 1968. Although no blood was shed during this coup, Saddam Hussein proved that he could be ruthless if need be. Surprisingly Saddam Hussein conducted himself as an effective and even progressive politician at the time. While holding that office, he modernized Iraq's infrastructure, improved the health-care system, raised social services, fomented education, created farming subsides. All which were policies that were in vanguard in and in contrast to any other Arab countries in the Region at the time. Saddam Hussein also nationalized Iraq's oil industry, which was well-timed before the 1973 energy crisis. The Nation received a lot of revenue.

But the constructive polices also came along with the bad. Saddam Hussein also was instrumental in the development of the first chemical weapons in Iraq. And this program was specifically created to protect the government against coups. Along with these, other authoritarian indicators sprouted such as the Ba'athist paramilitary groups and the People's Army. These groups were known for assassinations, torture, and raping as their frequent methods of control.

However, among authoritarians it is not a matter of if but when a scuffle would sprout to ultimately and dramatically change the status quo dynamic. In 1979 al-Bakr set the goal to unite Iraq and Syria, however this move would leave Saddam Hussein powerless.

On July 16, 1979, Saddam Hussein became Iraq's President after forcing al-Bakr to resign. Within a week he assembled the Ba'ath Party, where he infamously read out loud a list of 68 names while he was smoking a cigarette. As each person's name was being called out, they were arrested and removed from the assembly room. 22 of the men were sentenced to death, and all 68 were found guilty. The bloodshed continued with hundreds of his political enemies being executed by August 1979.

Think about this for a moment. For example, a nation's President entering their Congressional chamber and reading names of people who were somehow allied to him before, but no longer convenient to his power, and then security people would take down these now "inconvenient" politicians and kill them. That is what happened in Iraq!

1979 was quite a convoluted year. In Iran, Ayatollah Khomeini led what it was known as the Islamic Revolution and postulated himself as the supreme leader in Iraq's neighboring country. The Ayatollah follows the Shia version of Islam, while Saddam Hussein political power was aligned with the Sunni version of Islam. Saddam Hussein of course also saw this as a threat to his power based on these differences of Islamic interpretation. He was afraid that a similar Shia uprisal could occur in Iraq as it did in Iran. Also, it is worth mentioning that Shia and Sunni followers have a very long history of religious confrontations.

On September 22, 1980, Saddam Hussein invaded Iran, setting the target on the Khuzestan region which is rich in oil. This became an almost decade-long war. The rest of the world was also worried that the Ayatollah's influence would radicalize the rest of the Arab world and decided to back up Saddam Hussein despite him being the aggressor – in this case this was a clear violation of international law.

During this war the world also turned a blind eye to the fact that Iraq was using chemical weapons as they killed the Kurdish population in a genocidal manner. Saddam Hussein was also proposing a nuclear program. Finally on August 20, 1988, after leaving hundreds of thousands death on both sides, Iran and Iraq agreed to a ceasefire, but this is different from restoring peace.

As the 1980's decade was ending Saddam Hussein started a plot to invade Kuwait. His justification for this was his assertion that Kuwait was historically part of Iraq before they became an <u>independent</u> nation. Of course, that last part from the previous sentence is the crux of the issue, and what made it illegal to violate this country's sovereignty. On August 2, 1990, Saddam Hussein invaded this small oil-rich nation. The United Nations (UN) promptly imposed economic sanctions on Iraq and stipulated a deadline for Iraq to leave Kuwait. On January 15, 1991, Iraq blatantly disregarded the UNs deadline. That is when the UN coalition headed by the United States started a campaign against the Iraqi forces. The conflict lasted only six weeks, as the superior American military drove Iraq out of Kuwait. The result was a cease fire agreement that also required Iraq to dismantle their biological and chemical weapons programs.

This First Gulf War further polarized the Iraqi population. As the 1990's continued, new Kurdish and Shia uprises occurred. However, the rest of the world was not ready for a new war. Kurdish people were fighting for independence, but the fear of any Islamic fundamentalists thriving caused the world to leave the Kurdish to do the bulk of this fighting alone. We must understand that the lines in the map did not always look the same way as today, and Kurdish people were not only in the north of Iraq, but also populated a significant portion of Turkey.

Unsurprisingly, Saddam Hussein ultimately defeated the Kurdish rebels without much effort. Saddam Hussein, however, continued to commit violations of international law. Of note, a couple of those violations included the allegation of weapons programs and violation of no-fly zones. These eventually led to additional missile strikes into Iraq in 1998.

In January 2002, U.S. President George W. Bush named Iraq, Iran, and North Korea the "Axis of Evil" during his State of Union address. At this time, he claimed that Iraq was developing Weapons of Mass Destruction (WMD), to include nuclear weapons, and that this country was supporting terrorism. On the same year, UN inspectors searched Iraq and found no evidence of any nuclear WMDs. Surprise!

Regardless, on March 20, 2003, a US-led coalition invaded Iraq and within weeks the Iraqi government fell on April 9, 2003. This attack was under the pretense that WMDs did exist, and that Iraq planned on using them against the US.

Even though Bagdad fell, Saddam Hussein was able to escape, and released several audio recordings denouncing the coalition for invading Iraq and called for resistance. The answers to the calls never arrived. On December 13, 2003, Saddam Hussein was found hiding in a small bunker near Tikrit, his hometown. He was then transported to a U.S. Base in Bagdad until June 30, 2004. He was then officially turned to the interim Iraqi government where he stood trial for crimes against humanity. During the trial Saddam Hussein was belligerent and challenged this interim's government authority. On November 5, 2006, Saddam Hussein was found guilty and sentenced to death by Iraq's interim government. Saddam Hussein was hanged on December 30, 2005, at camp Justice, which is an Iraqi base in Baghdad. When sentenced to death, Saddam Hussein requested to be shot, this request was denied, and he was hanged instead.

After Saddam Hussein's death the country remained in conflict and instability for several years thereafter. There are no winners in this conflict. And it goes to show how the biases at different times in our history can play a determined role in the course of history. Even if the premise for those decisions was not based on sound logic or even facts. The events that forged Saddam Hussein's life, and subsequent time in power, were conflagrated with internal and external issues. Many of those were part of his own upbringing, many were cultural factors that were placed out of context by himself and others, and of course the biases from many nations that did not understand the culture and intricacies of the very lives that get affected under these collective decisions. Even if these intentions were well-intentioned.

*****

Idi Amin Dada | Uganda
Born 1925 (some accounts say 1928) – Died 16 AUG 2003 Died in a coma due kidney failure.

Regime in power from 1971 to 1979

Idi Amin Dada Oumee was born in Uganda. He was born in a tribe with Islamic influence. In fact, as a young boy, he had memorized sizable parts of the Quran. As he grew, he caught the attention of a British officer, and this started his entry into the British Colonial Army which started his military career. When he became a soldier, he was promoted rapidly and gained a reputation for obedience, brashness and even cruelty against the enemy. He was a gigantic man (size-wise) and considered by many a model soldier. As he raised through the ranks, he was able to make good on extreme threats against enemies, which even included as cutting off the male genitalia from adversaries. (Yeah, I know.)

Eventually Uganda gained independence from Great Britain. He was then given a high military position in the new government. When irregularities were found against him, he essentially just brushed over the claims. He even committed crimes against those looking into those allegations. In 1969 the Uganda congress was concerned about his galvanization of power. This unfortunately was when the brutality of his power started to terrorize the people from his own country. The Uganda's president was losing popularity, but Idi Amin was admired by great swats of Uganda's population. This became the catalyst for his dictatorship to get started. Even though he promised free elections, of course he was not in a hurry to do so. During that time, he even awarded himself some very bizarre titles such as "Lord of all beasts of the Earth and fishes of the sea" – I am serious, look it up.

In 1972, he expelled all Asians from the country. If they refused, they would face arrest or worse. This group was used as a scapegoat for political purposes. Whatever the Asian people left behind in Uganda was shared among Idi Amin's closest followers. Assassinations became routine, and private property was getting confiscated by the victims. Especially from any foreigners. Idi Amin became awfully close with Gadhafi in Libya and with Russia for weapons in a way to galvanize his stance against the West. At the same time there were a lot of dehumanizing dismembering and killings of political enemies occurring on a constant basis. He also killed all other army officers in Uganda and replaced them with goat herders who were loyal to his regime.

Half a million Uganda's citizens were killed. The primary targets were foreigners, teachers, doctors, lawyers, diplomats, and journalists. Unlike other dictators who left the dirty job of bloodying their hands to followers, Idi Amin took pleasure in brutalizing his victims directly. For example, he would torture people and feed their heads to crocodiles. He even claimed to have eaten the flesh from his enemies and kept their heads in a fridge (perhaps before feeding these heads to the crocodiles).

He diverted the taxes from the country into his expanding armed forces. As his paranoia grew, he established an enormous security detail who were also murderers. This group of loyalists grew as he dissolved any other powers of government giving himself unilateral power. The killings continued every day. He also acted in the international strata advocating severing all of Africa from Western influence.

The rest of the world was not oblivious to this madness. Idi Amin even barraged 200+ passengers who were hostages from a highjacked plane from Israel in 1976. The Israelites were able to rescue these hostages. He was very angry about this of course. Among other indicators from his misguided doctrines, he wanted to create a memorial to Hitler. During the first attempted coup against him in 1977 he killed them all.

During his regime, Idi Amin also made a preemptive attack to Tanzania, lying to the Ugandan people that Tanzania was planning an attack. This was a tactic to galvanize people's support as his popularity (unsurprisingly) was dwindling. The invasion to Tanzania was a failure. Tanzania not only fought back, but the Uganda locals united with Tanzania and started making their way against Idi Amin himself.

Idi Amin broadcasted to his people – particularly the army - to come to the rescue and fight for him. The people ignored these calls. Idi Amin and his five wives and 35 children fled to Libya. Because Uganda was in such bad shape after he left, his time in Libya was relatively carefree. This exile was finally the end to his brutal regime, though instability in Uganda sustained after he was gone. His country was left highly indebted. Also, he left behind hundreds of thousands of corpses of his own people. Idi Amid had a discord with Libyan Dictator Gadhafi in 1981 and moved to Saudi Arabia. Idi Amin and his family lived off handouts from the Saudi government.

Idi Amin tried to come back to Uganda in 1988 with some armed followers. He was unable to retake power. He eventually died of kidney failure after a coma. His family disconnected the life support to let him die with dignity. Idi Amin died in a Hospital in Saudi Arabia though he denied life or even a dignified death to hundreds of thousands of people.

*****

When it comes to authoritarian regimes. As you can see in the examples above the word "dictator" will show up often. Notice that most of these authoritarian figures were able to galvanize their power because they seized an opportunity. Generally, people were upset about something. If there was a controversy that negatively affected their national pride, likely a lot of the followers would be willing to "listen" because these authoritarian figures seemed to have a "solution."

However, the solution was not ultimately a win-win scenario. In every example, anybody who was not onboard their program would be eliminated in any available way. Their methods of execution and dehumanization continued to evolve. As in every example in world history, very rarely the authoritarian himself or herself would be doing the bulk of the crimes against humanity directly. Though they would be the mastermind who would conceive these directives, or even condone and mandate these crimes. However, in every case it would ultimately be somebody subordinate to them who would enact or be complicit to those acts of cruelty and other atrocities.

Please do not be deceived by the dates on these regimes as something that only happened in the past. There are several authoritarian regimes in existence at the time I am typing this manuscript. Some of these could be even closer to you than what you have realized. Some might seem as though they have infiltrated daily life as a benevolent force. Or might even look very tolerant on the surface, but their people are subjugated in ways they might not even realize. The very propaganda-style that helped these authoritarians raise and keep power is pushed onto everyday people all the time.

For example, an authoritarian regime is likely tracking their population's every move. This tracking can be as simple as having people following them. Or they can be as high tech as surveillance using their own smart devices, and even face recognition cameras in many public areas. This technology exists. And though this convenient technology can be utilized to do something beneficial such as helping you unlock your phone or tablet, or even do some cashless transactions – which is by the way possibly the primary use for this technology; it can also be used to keep tabs on people and utilize this data for whatever reason people of influence in that regime decide they want to use it for later.

As you can imagine, some of those uses can afford nefarious intent and actions. Particularly on political enemies or any other dissenting actors. The difference between the regimes we spoke of in the past in this chapter and the one in modern times is technology. Also, and paradoxically because of this technology, there is a sense of complacency and lowering our guards. In other words, a lot of people overshare information in social media, or in any other medium they have available. Do you think this information is safe from scrutiny by a nefarious actor? It is not, anything you say could or will be recorded somehow and by somebody if there is any way to collect such information. Especially if this information is transmitted via the internet.

This is something we take for granted. We are led to believe that everything we do in our browser's history is being kept private. It is not, and it could be intercepted if somebody really wants to get into it. Your information and mine has probably been compromised by somebody without us even knowing or being aware of it. That is why I will not mention any current authoritarian regime by name.

The rationale is as follows. If an authoritarian regime decides to ban my book or my words today or at any time in their history, even though they were never mentioned by name; then that is *their* tacit acknowledgment and agreement that the regime they lead is indeed authoritarian. Which means that the burden of proof about my words attacking their regime will fall on them. Not just in the court of public opinion, but in the annals of history. The truth ultimately comes to light, sometimes in unexpected ways – even if it takes centuries. But spoiler alert, I am not speaking about any one authoritarian regime. I am talking about the formula they all have followed in one way or the other.

And another spoiler, a traditionally democratic government could turn into authoritarianism given several factors. And I said factors, because they become multipliers in order to galvanize certain amounts of followers to enact their agendas.

And why am I saying that the truth can come after years in unexpected manners? Well, for instance because of technology. For example, DNA analysis has been able to clear the names of people who were condemned of a crime they did not commit. Also, as information becomes available and factors and patterns become clearer, then new pieces of a puzzle can unlock other leads. I am of course oversimplifying for the sake of brevity – but the point is that as time moves forward some things that were once a mystery eventually get solved. In either case, critical thinking and pragmatism in the analysis is what helps to solve these cases. We will talk more about that in the next chapter.

CHAPTER 7

CRITICAL THINKING |
The Real Freedom

The name of the game for today's society is <u>attention</u>.
Somebody is fighting to get your attention every moment of the day. Attention is prime real estate, and I appreciate you taking the time to pay attention to my words as you read this book.
There are entire industries that are based on our attention, and most importantly turning this attention into a tangible result. Whatever the result might be. Normally to try selling you something, but in the case of the authoritarians it is to turn that attention into a visceral response that will result in action. The way they can achieve this is by attacking your critical thinking and painting a false reality in your mind. Critical thinking without understanding context will potentially lead to skewed conclusions.
The way you can gain this context is by enacting <u>Intellectual Honesty</u>. That will help you realize what you know, and what you do not know. And, most importantly, learn how whatever you do not know could affect your decision making. As you read these words, I will give you the biggest gift I can think of, the <u>Real Freedom</u> of proper critical thinking and intellectual honesty.

Critical thinking is one of those overused terms, and often used erroneously. Most people confuse critical thinking with dissention and skepticism, respectively. And although critical thinking could lead to dissention and skepticism, those terms are not synonymous with one another. However, if somebody with an agenda wants to push pomposity onto unsuspecting followers, they will muddy the waters. This will create a visceral response on the target audience and subsequently the propagandist will be able to manipulate these people into following them.

How obediently, or how fast will they follow this agenda? It will depend on the person, and the skill level of the propagandist. In some instances, the seeds are planted years ahead of the actual intended action. For example, there are regimes that have and are indoctrinating children. These children will grow up learning these indoctrination teachings as empirical truths – and in some instances making it their duty and purpose in life to follow.

And we are all vulnerable to these agendas, if we are not careful. It works like this:

We all have a bias. A bias is a pre-conceived notion for or against something or someone we prefer over something or someone we feel as their opposite. These biases could be religious, political, organizational or any other type of preference we seem to favor towards a person, ideology, entity, etc.

For example, we might have a bias towards our own children, and see them in a more positive light than the children of others. Or this bias could be reversed, and we might tend to see other children as better behaved or higher achieving than our own kids. It can work both ways. There is going to be some leaning towards one side or the other, and it is in this leaning where our mind can get in the way of our critical thinking.

These are in essence logical fallacies based on perceptions or misperceptions. There could be some merit to the reason why we reach these fallacies, such as events that seem to validate this perception. I was just talking to some people today about a term that we use in the U.S. Navy that I absolutely hate: "Perception is reality" – I hate that because it is a logical fallacy.

Perception is _not_ reality. We perceive reality through our senses, and our senses are fallible. Our impressions of something are fallible, and our own biases could skew that reality dramatically. What seems obvious to one person based on the factors that encompass their persona, might be very different to another person who does not share the same factors. These factors could be anything that the person has experienced, and it is considered correct and proper in <u>their</u> environment, but it would not be considered adequate in a different environment.

Let me give you an example. This will be a bit of a philosophical exercise. Let us say that in a culture where there is a hot and humid climate the people native to that place will wear little to no clothing. There would be no shame, objectification, nor anything "disgusting" nor inappropriate about their attire – because it makes sense to them not to have to be wrapped in fabric in a hot and humid environment. But now, let us say that this group is visited by people who were raised in a very different culture. And for them if it gets hot their clothing might be composed of lighter fabrics, and perhaps short sleeves and shorts, but in their mind covering "their modesty." Which group is choosing the right attire?

Short answer, both. If the people who come over and decide to wear an outfit that seems to work for them in this hot and humid environment and it is not disrespectful to the other group, then that is fine. Correct?

Let us think about this: so far, the visiting group are not forcing these natives on their own land to cover up more than what the natives consider acceptable, then it should be fine. In other words, if you do not like that, then do not go visit them. But hey, maybe the natives will enjoy the feel of the fabric and the way these clothes fit them. Or perhaps they will hate how the fabrics feel now that the perspiration is causing the clothes to cling to their skin. Maybe they hate the restrictiveness of the fabric.

But in both cases, these clothing options could seem appropriate for that climate. The visitors came to the land where the status quo was for the natives to wear less of what they chose to wear. There is nothing inherently wrong with that.

But now, let us turn the tables around and these natives are invited to visit these other people's community. Everybody else in this other society will dress much like the group who came to visit the natives with shorts and short sleeves but otherwise very conservatively. But the same climate. So, what if the natives who are now visiting decide that they want to wear *their own* attire that they enjoy back at home in this other part of the world? What would be the reaction among the "natives" from this other area where traditional clothes are the norm? Think about it for a second, just try to visualize the circumstances as the visitors appear before the natives, and the natives appear before the people not native to this area.

Should the natives visiting this more traditional population be forced to wear the clothes of the place they are visiting? Is that acceptable? Why? Remember that these natives did not force their dress code onto the other visitors.

"Modesty" and repression have come hand in hand for centuries. Some cultures have sexualized the human body to such a point that any semblance of immodesty is correlated with leud behavior, and even equated as shameful...and for some religious groups, sinful. But spoiler alert, the human body is not inherently sexual nor is it shameful. It has been sexualized over the years because of the repressions that have been imposed in many societies.

For the natives in this example, they were not sexualizing their bodies therefore their choice of attire (or lack thereof) was more of a practical use. However, for the minds of others who are not used to seeing these exposed bits of skin, these mere thoughts were enough to create a reaction. A reaction that could be described as sexualized. Why do you think that is?

Because in most societies, nudity is erroneously exclusive to the correlation with sex. And I am using this example because I know that it will spark the curiosity of some people as they try to think about what I am saying. I could have very well used an example about dichotomies in environmental laws, and that might have painted a much different picture than the example that I chose. But I digress. Let us get back on topic.

For some people, the mere thought of disrobing in a social setting would be taboo. For some it would be no big deal, while for others it might be very exciting. And I am sure there would be other reactions, and combinations of any of those. However, I just want to help turn the mind's wheels with the fact that what we consider normal and acceptable is not necessarily what is the norm for everybody. It is the product of our environment. In other words, our biases.

There is an entire gamma of thoughts and responses that can be exploited. Ideally, for a propagandist, they will find in their target audience some sort of bias that will make it easier for them to wake up a response in their followers. It does not matter what the response is or even what the topic they have chosen to get that response. It can be saving the children, save the planet, religious prosecution, climate change, deep state, conspiracy theories, gas prices, renewable energy, fossil fuels, Android vs Apple, MAC vs Windows, Roe vs Wade, Republicans vs Liberals… again it does not matter. The goal is to find what attention-grabbing technique will be the most fertile vehicle to keep pushing more rhetoric onto them.

As the propagandists keep feeding more information on each bias, then the propagandists can paint a different reality into the follower's minds. In other words, give them more of what they are already convinced is right – even if they are wrong. Nobody enjoys being told they are wrong about something, especially if it is a topic near and dear to their heart. Therefore, the more natural response is to gravitate towards whomever seems to agree with our own biases. Get enough content to convince people that their biases are 100% justified, then they will be willing to turn that rhetoric into action.

The human mind is not static, it is a dynamic environment. And critical thinking requires training our minds in order to separate facts from unsubstantiated opinions. For some people it will be quite easy, and for some it will take a longer time. But remember what I said before – critical thinking without intellectual honesty is not going to work very well. Some people who have critical thinking but lack intellectual honesty can become actual victims of their own biases. Their own cynicism will blind them from actual reality, because getting outside those boundaries will feel as though they are defying their very logic.

Have you ever seen two people argue about something that they are both wrong about? But in their mind, they are *both* convinced that they are right. Is it not amusing to witness when they try to defend their point of view with platitudes and circular reasoning? And yes, some of those examples could include religion and politics, but it can really be anything else. Let us say, for example, that they are arguing about which band is famous for the song, "Living on a Prayer." One of them would erroneously assert that it was *REO Speedwagon,* and the other would say – also erroneously – that it is *Poison w*hen, in reality, it is a *Bon Jovi* song. True story, by the way. And you should have seen how adamant and convinced these two guys were. Both were even spouting names, and dates, etc. It was hilariously tragic.

By the way, that was back in the early 90's so we did not have a chance to do a quick Google search. I did, however, show them my very own cassette, *Bon Jovi "Slippery When Wet"* album featuring the song, "Living on a Prayer." Which I just so happened to have in my "Walkman" at that time. One of them still argued that it was not possible and that he was right with zero proof for his claim. Even though I made them both hear the song playing in my Walkman on an official cassette, clearly showing the title of the song and artist printed in said cassette.

For anybody who does not know what a Walkman is, it was a little portable cassette player. And a cassette was a little cartridge of magnetic tape that was spooled with audio tape, generally storing about an hour's worth of songs, or so. And if you wanted to listen to a specific song, you needed to rewind the tape to an estimated place on the tape where the song was saved. The quality was *meh,* but that is what was available back then. The struggle was real. Some of you young souls will never have to deal with that.

In either case, that is an example of circular reasoning I have seen earlier in my life. Some people will be so convinced about a certain "reality" that it does not matter how much empirical evidence you show to them. They will do all sorts of mental gymnastics to make it fit their assertion as the correct one – even if there are different demonstrable sciences that can debunk such claims. And that is what I am saying – critical thinking alone is not enough. In order to break free, a person also needs intellectual honesty in order to understand the difference between reality and falsehoods. Especially when they might have originally <u>chosen</u> to believe the wrong doctrines.

Let me give you a couple of examples. There are people out there who think that the world is flat. It is <u>not</u> flat. Yet, there is an entire society – the Flat Earth Society – whose entire premise is that the world is flat AND that the Earth is part of a related global conspiracy. They go on to say that the world's edges are a gigantic wall of ice that is guarded by military people. In other words, Antarctica is the big wall of ice that surrounds the circumference of "this disk" that they think we all live upon. Among other claims is that they seem convinced that the sun and the moon are a lot smaller and a lot closer to Earth than they really are.

And what is funny – and tragic – at the same time is that they will try to use "science" to prove their erroneous point. And for anybody who understands actual science, they will be able to see these claims are very lacking in, both, substance and merits. But that does not matter to those believers. They are critically thinking about these options given the skewed data, and ignoring data that conflicts with *their* <u>perception</u> of reality. See why I hate the term "perception is reality?" For flat-earthers, this belief of the world being flat is very real to *them*.

But the flat-earthers are not alone in history about the erroneous assertion of a flat Earth. Many religious dogmas and other cultures felt the same way because they did not understand the different variables that would debunk that claim.

Today, the flat-earthers are not the only group that will find quasi-scientifically, and frankly quasi-logical geographical phenomena because of their skewed preconceptions. Another classic example is another group of people who think the Grand Canyon was created in about a week due to the flood described in several bible versions. You know, the one in the book of Genesis where Noah and his family rounded up a bunch of animals on an arc and floated for a very long time after their God grew mad at mankind and killed everything by flooding the entire surface of Earth, with the obvious exception of the riders who were safely onboard this wooden vessel.

Regardless of any of our convictions or beliefs on biblical allegories, the Grand Canyon took several million years to be carved into what it is today. In fact, as I type this manuscript the oldest rocks in the canyon are about 1,840 million years old, but the carving is relatively young. Geologically speaking, it is about six million years. And yes, that is a lot longer than a week. Indeed, a lot of religious people have reconciled this reality with their religious doctrines.

With that being said, there are plenty of people who will defend this erroneous claim. But the reason is because it would conflict with a religious bias. And we must admit that religious biases are enormously powerful in the sense that they would create a "blockade" in the person's mind. In other words, if there is a conflicting fact or set of facts then these will become taboo or denied outright without giving them enough scrutiny on the merits. Why? Because religious beliefs are deeply engrained in a lot of people, and some of those engrained beliefs make the very thought of setting a belief into scrutiny a sinful, sacrilegious, or blasphemous offense. And that can scare the living crap out of people who are very much convinced that their religious view is the one and only true doctrine. Even if it is only one among the thousands of religious doctrines that exist – or have existed – as I write these words.

And I know that talking about religion can be a volatile topic. But we must also remember that religions were developed to be volatile for a reason. To ensure their followers would defend their faith to their last breath. In other words, convince them that any level of scrutiny – however small – is an attack on their faith. What happens next is a very interesting physiological response.

People who are very devoted to their faith – whichever one that they practice – will feel <u>physically</u> hurt if someone questions *their* beliefs. This is especially evident if their faith is not only a personal identifier, but it is also a collective and community unifier. What do I mean by that? Look at a world map and point at any random country other than yours. There is a chance that a random country has worshiped or is currently worshiping a deity that might be very different than yours. And if you question their beliefs, they might feel very offended, or will kill you for insulting their faith. In actuality, this does happen in the world from time to time, and it has been happening for centuries.

Religious practices have been with humanity for as long as we have been roaming the planet. There has been some sort of belief. Some cultures worshiped natural phenomena such as the sun, the moon, or even the wind. Some would worship geological sites such as a volcano, rivers, or mountains. Some would worship animals such as snakes, cows, etc. Some would worship one god, some would worship several gods, some would worship no gods at all – but instead worship a collective consciousness. Some will worship their deceased. The fact is that their society could have been practicing devotion to one religion or deity. It does not matter if others outside this group have been worshiping something totally contrary. But for each one of those devotees the feelings will be very real. There are people who will enter trances based on their faith. However, even these forms of worship would be considered heretical to practitioners from other faiths.

And holy wars occur even to this day. Do you know who loves when people galvanize their faith for unabashed obedience? Authoritarians. No surprise there. Authoritarians very well know that religion is an enormously powerful motivator. And they have been using it since the very beginning. And why shouldn't they? It makes any additional doctrine modification more palatable if it is settled on a basis the followers already respect and follow. In other words, religion offers a strong bias they can exploit effectively and with relative ease.

With this I am not asking you to leave your faith, or worse attack <u>your</u> faith, or whichever belief you practice and profess to. What I am telling you is that religion – all religions – are indeed a bias. And if we lose objectivity based on our religious convictions, there might be a blind spot somebody is going to exploit for their own benefit. Intellectual honesty comes from the fact that you must ask yourself if you're willing to accept that risk. But that also would imply that you would also give unequivocal opportunity to people who subscribe to a different faith to assume the very <u>same</u> risk. Are you willing to do so if *their* faith conflicts with yours? If you can, then you are intellectually honest. If you cannot, then your biases could be exploited and subject you to manipulation.

Salvation and eternal damnation are very powerful rhetorical vehicles that could also find their way into political doctrines. That is one of the reasons why in countries such as the United States of America – despite many Christians calling it a Christian nation – was indeed founded with the separation of church and state.

Why? Because the next logical follow up question would be <u>which</u> religion should be a national religion and why? So, for those that are under the assertion that Christianity should be the religion of the land, then there is another logical follow up question. Which <u>denomination</u> from the thousands in the Christian religion is the correct one? I'm sure that not every Christian would be happy if they were assigned a specific denomination that they do not subscribe to. Especially if it is the one that becomes the national religion. Are you willing to be an all-Catholic country? What about an all Pentecostal? Or a Latter-Day Saints? Or Jehovah Witness? Or Episcopalian? Or one of the many Baptist denominations? Or Calvinist? What about making prosperity gospel the law of the land? Why not? Aren't all the denominations that I mentioned examples of Christianity? Yes, they are! But they all disagree on doctrinal practices. And wars and crimes against humanity have been largely fought over due to those differences. As I said before, religion forms a strong bias.

The scary thing is that these types of biases would have the followers feel empowered and even vindicated in the enforcing of their doctrines. That is true for any practitioners, as well to any non-practitioner. For example, during the time of the Inquisition the Vatican endorsed terrible and perverse crimes against humanity. These crimes were perpetrated against non- believers and suspected sinners. And we are talking about brutal and disfiguring torture as well as horrendous painful killings. All in the name of *their oppressor's* faith. And these torturers would feel vindicated and anointed to follow a divine mandate – because that is what the Vatican leadership convinced them was the right thing to do.

But we must remember that morals do not come from any religious text. Although religious believers would assert otherwise. But it is really a lot simpler than that. It is all about the golden rule. Treat others as you would like to be treated. In other words, be nice to others so they will hopefully be nice to you too. But if you want others to mistreat you, then you can achieve that by mistreating them. Hopefully nobody wants to be mistreated. But, then again, it is a big world out there full of ridiculous schools of thought with many that don't make a lot of sense to me, yet there they are.

For something to make sense it needs to be logical, measurable, and demonstrable. If it cannot meet this simple trifecta, then it is conjecture. The math is not going to add up somewhere. That is why intellectual honesty is needed. Some tend to push a logical fallacy as assertion that their claim is factual. But then it cannot be measurable or demonstrable. For example, if it is unfalsifiable, then you know that there is essentially no way to prove that point to be true or not. That does not automatically mean that the subject for claim does not exist. But exceptional claims require exceptional evidence. If evidence, either concrete or abstract such as a practical mathematical formula cannot be produced, then the burden of proof is on whomever is making the claim. Why? Because you cannot prove a negative.

Whomever is making the claim is the one who carries the burden of proof for their claim.

Propagandists will push circular reasoning because it is more convenient to have their followers believe a doctrine based on a logical fallacy, such as an argument for authority or an argument for ignorance or straw-manning, rather than using empirical facts to prove their claim without a shadow of a doubt.

And yes, churches and other religious leaders have been instrumental throughout history in pushing propaganda. As I mentioned before, in the United States of America there is a separation of church and state. In fact, the policy supporting religions' tax exemption mandates that religious leaders are not to push political rhetoric to their congregations. Are non- political biases getting pushed from the pulpit rule enforced in the United States of America as I type this manuscript? Absolutely not.

The United States of America, although secular in The Constitution, has an exceptionally large religious following. A following that has been dwindling more and more, nonetheless.

And of course, a lot of religious leaders are freaking out about it. Why? Because religion is also a source of livelihood to millions of Americans, particularly due to the collection of tithes. For anybody who is not familiar with this term it comes from Old English, meaning 1/10. In other words, parishioners must contribute 10% of their income (after taxes) to *their* church. For you eagle-eyed people, you are correct. That means one month and one week's worth of a yearly salary, at a minimum. Though it is characterized as *voluntary*, it is quite a commitment. The question many have asked is: Do you "have to give 10%" of your after-tax income? And the answer was interesting. "You don't *have* to give 10%, you can always give *more*." That was a direct quote.

For many people, even those reading this book, they will characterize their tithe as fair and acceptable. And if it works for them, more power to them. I am not advocating against it – if people want to freely contribute 10% or more of their earnings to their church. What I am saying is that all of this income is tax free to the churches with the condition that they avoid involving their congregations in politics. In the sense that they are not supposed to influence or mandate their parishioners to vote or follow any political figure from the pulpit. That pushing of politics, as I said, are technically illegal in the United States of America.

The problem is that it does happen. And quite overtly, if I might add. There is no shortage of pastors – particularly some more controversial ones – who will not only advocate for a particular political figure, but even demonize anybody who is voting or in any way is providing support against their candidate of choice. And they will even feel entitled to defiantly state that they are politically influencing their congregation towards, and against, particular political doctrines or people.

And these politics that are being pushed from the pulpit also happen around the world. During World War II, the Pope was very tolerant when it came to the extermination of Jewish people, as well as any other victims in the concentration camps. Mussolini, who was the Italian dictator circa that time was able to galvanize the power of the Catholic Church in order to legitimize his support along with the Nazis. And, yes, the Nazis were allies with the Fascists during that conflict because both of these authoritarian figures were aligned against the rest of the world.

But going back to the political rhetoric in houses of worship, my recommendation is that if they want to push political rhetoric in a house of worship – they can do it. But that means that they must pay taxes like everybody else. Simple. If they want to keep their tax exception, then profess their religious doctrines and only their religious doctrines – which is, by the way, what they are supposed to be doing. There is a reason why religions should not push or advertise political rhetoric. Why? Because it can provide undue visceral influence on their congregation, especially if – for whatever reason – the information pushed from the pulpit is divorced from empirical reality. That is why there is separation of church and state.

But, of course, this is a prickly part where critical thinking and lack of intellectual honesty will hit a brick wall. It also makes sense why. Since this is a visceral topic, it would become contentious. And if there was any actual talk of disagreement, some would falsely accuse this questioning as prosecution. Which is not prosecution because everything in this world is subject to scrutiny. Checks and balances. That does not mean that an idea or person is being prosecuted. That misconstruction also creates a fertile ground for any charlatan to use the guise of religious freedom to push some crazy agendas.

For example, there are actual religious leaning people who claim that exotic animals are not real. I was laughing yesterday after hearing about this guy (who I will not name – I am not going to give this dude a platform to keep spewing nonsense – but you can Google that yourself) asserting that koala bears in Australia are actual animatronics, that zebras are donkeys who are painted with white and black stripes, and that platypuses are a hoax. I think he was also skeptical about sharks being real.

So, you see – skepticism and critical thinking does not necessarily mean that a person is making a viably coherent argument. In fact, this person was so wrong about these assertions that, at first, I thought he was just a troll. But no, he has a bunch of people following his every word as empirical fact. And, of course, he is using this rationale to try to reconcile this fantasy with his own religious biases.

To be honest, I think that is dangerous. I am from the school of thought that a serious and mature conversation about religion and politics is well overdue. Right now, there are several political extremists around the world who have very prominent religious biases. Some of these extremist biases have called for violence to any dissenting opposition. That includes people, organizations, countries, communities, etc. There are a lot of calls for subjugation of others under these religious mandates. And that is not something that should be tolerated as a possibility. What do I mean by that?

If you are a person of strong faith, would you be ok with a different religion becoming the ruling doctrine in the land and taking over you and your life? If you are, then your own current faith is not strong enough, as it will easily be exchanged by this imposition. If you are a secular person, then I am quite sure that you would not be ok with *any* faith being imposed onto you. Especially because plenty of atheists used to be people of faith who left their religion behind for many reasons.

Why do I keep talking about religion in this chapter? Because critical thinking and faith can be at odds with each other if the level of scrutiny hits this particular nerve. As I said before, people tend to suffer if they find their faith is being questioned – and worse, if the dissenting opinion makes sense. This can be a terrifying situation to them. Especially if they have a vested interest in it. For example, my mother, my father, all my grandparents, my friends, my in-laws, my community, they all went to the same church with me… we all grew up with this community… they cannot all be wrong? Can they?

When we can confront our "most sacred" convictions head on, then we are able to open our minds in the right manner. Some will assert that their mind is part of whatever deity they subscribe to. I will be brutally honest with you – no omnipotent deity needs YOU or any other person to assert their omnipotence. Any omnipotent deity should be able to validate himself, or herself, or itself, unequivocally and unambiguously on his, her, or its own.

And if you find that the math does indeed add up, and holding your deity to scrutiny led you to the same result your congregation unequivocally described, then live happy ever after for being able to truly validate that whatever you feel true within your heart ALSO aligns with the empirical evidence no matter the source. If you cannot do that on your own, please understand that you cannot expect others to figure it out for themselves and whatever it is you could not prove for yourself to be true.

I will make it easier for you. A simple equation is 1+3=4. Go ahead, and scrutinize that equation all you want, the result will be 1+3=4. Even if you break it differently:

1+1+1+1=4

2x2=4

2+1+1=4

3+1=4

2+2=4

Demonstrating that your deity is real should not be more ambiguous than this simple equation, even if you want to rationalize that every variation of the equation is a different denomination. Then the math does not add up as originally described – "1+3=4" – because the individual values do not all agree on what actual path leads to "4." Solve this equation and you will gain the freedom to understand critical thinking, skepticism, dissent, and the ultimate freedom of thought. You will see why this context is important in the next chapter.

CHAPTER 8

PAIN AND SUFFERING |
WARNING Explicit Content

WARNING – the language in this chapter will be extremely graphic and should not be read unless you have understood well the lessons in the earlier chapters. If you continue reading, please remember that this was your own choice. We are going to talk about horrific crimes against humanity.
There will be no pictures nor illustrations for the events we will discuss. However, you are more than welcome to do more research on your own about each event. There are plenty of archives – which include images – available on the internet. The purpose of this chapter is to work in conjunction with the previous chapter on critical thinking. This is why thinking critically will hopefully prevent people from becoming instruments of inflicting pain and suffering onto others. There is no shortage of barbaric crimes against humanity in our history. And yes, crimes against humanity are occurring even as I am typing this manuscript. But remember, the crimes were perpetrated by an actual obedient follower, regardless of who issued the order to commit the atrocities. Read it with an open mind because this is the reality of our world. Again, some readers might find these descriptions disturbing.

Human beings are paradoxical creatures. For example, we can create immense beauty through art. We, as a species through technology, have been capable of leaving the confines of our planet and venturing into space. Even though humans have stepped only as far as our own moon, we are even able to intercept asteroids with our technology. In fact, human-made spacecrafts have landed on planets and moons farther than any human being could ever walk in this lifetime. There are amazing minds capable of calculating extremely complex data and providing solutions that until very recently would have been considered magical, or even impossible. Science and technology continue to advance in ways that are beyond what some of our science fiction imagination could have predicted. Yet, even today, we are living in a world of willful ignorance where we are killing one another because there are some people – or too many – who refuse to be objective and intellectually honest. I will focus on a particular group from this vast number of people for the purpose of this chapter. The obedient fools.

These obedient fools have been responsible for some of the worst crimes in world history. They have existed since the beginning of civilization. They will be the *muscle* behind the authoritarian. They will be, and have been, the errand boys and girls who will get their hands bathed in blood in the name of *their* "dear leader."

And worse, some of these obedient fools even enjoyed inflicting this power and dehumanization over others. We are going to explore the very dark, yet real side of our human species. Some of this will come to you as a surprise. Some of these you might've heard about at some point in your life. In either case the capacity to inflict pain and suffering is not only a tale of the old days. Unfortunately, this happens in this day and age, and the brutal consequences are not limited to rivalries, but they span many innocent victims around the world. Many of these victims will be dehumanized without even knowing the cruelty that awaits them.

In a prominent segment of cruelty enablers throughout history we have religions. Yes, religion and their deities are the leading cause of death and suffering to millions. And I am not talking about one religion. Religious rituals and practices have been linked to unspeakable cruelty. Sure, you might think that y<u>ou</u>r congregation in *your* little corner of the world is a wholesome group of devoted good people. Sure, I will give you that. It could very well be that *your* congregation is wholesome, and they advocate for the good of mankind. But we are not talking about you (hopefully). We are talking about the millions of other individuals who have used their deity as a direct advocate and condoning catalyst for punishing those who would be considered enemies of their doctrines.

The Holocaust during World War II was religiously motivated. Christian, in fact – sorry. Not all Christians are terrible people, but these terrible people happened to be Christians. And these Christians were not only the Nazis, but they also had a bunch of other Europeans who worked along with the Nazis in the extermination and dehumanization of millions of Jewish people.

Did you know that Jewish people were not the only ones who got exterminated by the Nazis? They also rounded up and killed homosexuals, people with mental health issues, Romani people (Gypsies), political enemies, prisoners of war, defectors, minorities, etc. And when we are talking about dehumanizing it was horrific. The divisive rhetoric that was rampant in the years leading to war – it was truly dehumanizing. This series of violent events did not happen overnight. But rather it took a while to galvanize these sentiments in the minds of the people who would not only sanction this behavior but would turn the rhetoric into horrific actions. In other words, there are usually some indicators to learn if a potential violence-driven trend is growing.

The most startling truth is that everybody is capable of immense savagery if <u>persuaded</u> enough. This is the dark side of the human psyche. Even the nicest person can get extremely angry. Even the most loving person can harbor hate in their heart. They might not know it, but it could come up if the circumstances are such that these darker sentiments will surface and change their very essence.

This could also be repressed, or even "forbidden" by the faith they happen to practice, but it is there. Why? Because these feelings are attributed as a human trait, not a religious one. Sure, some people will take much longer than others to deal with any animosity that consumes them inside. That will also depend on many intrinsic factors about their personality, coped with the extrinsic factors that make them the person they are today. In simpler terms, people are complex, and their decisions will ultimately be dictated as the culmination of their experiences.

A bias could be forged from these experiences, even unconsciously. A bias is an exploitable factor, as I mentioned before. But there is a lot more to than what meets the eye. Have you heard before the trope that "money changes people for the worse?" Money does not necessarily change people, what it does is allows people to get away with stuff that they could not get away with before they had the financial means. Sometimes for the better, sometimes for the worse. In other words, money alone is not going to make somebody a nasty person. That means that this person was already callous, but now this is a callous person with money. That is the main difference. Some advantages will worsen certain bad behaviors because they give additional power and reach to their misguided escapades.

Same thing with people who achieve a certain rank or position. If they are callous already, they will use this additional power as a tool to get away with whatever is possible under that power construct. The higher the position, the higher the abuse of authority. This is not new and has been happening for millennia. And as bad as that is it can get worse.

Some of these toxic personalities find a fertile following of like-minded individuals. The most disturbing thing is that these group of followers are individuals who are already predisposed to follow directives that could require the "enforcing" of certain rules through violence and intimidation. These are the loyal followers, and useful fools who are the de facto obedient fools. The muscle needed to continue the authoritarian's will.

And to add insult to injury, many of these blind followers will pray and give grace to their own deity before, during, and after they commit crimes against humanity. Because they are convinced that their actions are justified by their interpretation of whatever sacred doctrine they follow. Particularly if this doctrine was perpetuated by their respected authority figure. For example, the Mayans would have religious events and some of the events would require the brutal assassination of a human being in the name of their god's will. Of course, sometimes this human sacrifice was portrayed as an honor. Oh, what an honor – to be the young person chosen and later be brutally murdered in front of a crowd atop of a pyramid or in one of the many other manners Mayans offered sacrifices to their Gods.

And speaking about the human psyche, it has been reported by some accounts that the actual victims could even feel elated about being brutally executed – if they were convinced this was a worthy cause for their impending sacrifice. We will not know how they felt for sure because they are dead. Dead people do not talk directly.

Let us use the case of suicide bombers as an example. To them, this type of martyrdom was viewed as an occasion to serve, not only their society in what they considered a worthy cause, but also for rewards in the afterlife. In many cases, these levels of indoctrination started incredibly early in life. Children as young as they can start speaking and believing in their dogmas are conditioned to carry these acts of "martyrdom" as though they are the *chosen ones* for their cause. It is macabrely cynical, especially when you come to realize that the higher echelons of leadership do not do the suicidal martyrdom themselves. I know, right? Surprisingly, the people in charge do zero sacrificial dying themselves, huh? Why do you think that is? Isn't this supposed to be the greatest honor? Afterall, they conditioned and convinced this poor soul to believe that it was an honor by bombing themselves and their targets.

But then again, there are some dear leaders who will commit suicide and take along as many of their followers and enemies as possible to their graves just for the dying frenzy.

For the record, it is not an honor. Depriving any other person of their life is not something anybody should take as a matter of celebration. And I know that I am saying this even though capital punishment for people who had committed atrocities is an option many countries have adopted throughout the years. However, in more civilized societies, the inevitable execution of a person found guilty of heinous crimes is supposed to be conducted in a humane way. And I am not trying to justify any monsters who perpetrated heinous crimes. Especially if they killed another person in a way that maximized the victim's suffering and agony for some sort of sick pleasure. There are very twisted people out there.

This book is not an argument for, or against, capital punishment. But what I will say is that plenty of people who were found guilty, tried, and executed were proven innocent postmortem. What is the moral liability for a state-sanctioned murder if the person the state killed was, in fact, innocent? Not just for the killing, but the entire confinement leading to death row. Food for thought.

Even in the event that the person was, in fact, guilty under the premise for capital punishment, this is not intended to match brutality on a state-sponsored execution. I know this has been a matter of debate and people who had committed unspeakable crimes do not earn [in the court of public opinion] the benefit of being treated fairly after they denied the existence of another human being. There is going to be a visceral response to these cases, and some people might even feel enticed to take matters into their own hands. In fact, look to your left or your right – somebody is possibly carrying a weapon that could end your life and the life of those around you today if the "provocation seems justified." And, yes, this happens more often than it should.

Let me give you an example. The United States of America has one of the highest numbers of murder in the world. Every other day we have mass shootings. And with this, I am not arguing about American's 2nd Amendment rights. Though some of the same people who defend the 2nd Amendment will not be able to tell me from the top of their head what the 7th Amendment is, which is "The right of citizen's cases to be heard and decided upon by a jury of their peers".

However, they will be very aware of the existence of the 2nd Amendment as it has a lot of political baggage and, with that, a sizable amount of marketing. This argument has even percolated itself into a lot of religious congregations. As a result, we have more guns than inhabitants on this country. That does not mean that everybody owns a firearm, it means that a few own a whole bunch of them.

And I know this is a sensitive issue to a lot of Americans. Particularly the trigger-happy ones. Let me be clear, I am not against people being able to buy and carry a firearm if that is what they desire. What I am advocating for is common sense regulation – and most of the country agrees with that. And yes, this is realizing that felons will not obey rules (and that is a red herring argument). We still require driver licenses, age limits, and insurance requirements to own and operate a vehicle. That does not mean that some people will not drive without a license or insurance. But it does legally protect those who are driving within the sensible guidelines when it comes to driving and using a vehicle.

One of the most watered-down arguments I keep hearing is that a firearm is nothing but a tool. Yes, but it is a tool specifically designed to kill or produce substantial bodily harm to another living being. You can technically kill a person with a spoon, or with a car, or even by shanking them with a pen, but all those other tools I mentioned were not specifically designed to kill.

So, then the next logical question on the firearms availability is, what is the purpose for this purchase? Is it for self-defense? Is it for sport? Is it for pleasure? Is it for display? Is it simply part of a collection? Sure, it is your choice and a right to spend your money on getting these *tools*. But in any case, what is their intended use? What were they specifically designed to do?

The reality is that most times if somebody buys something it is because they intend to use it somehow at some point. Likely in the way that it was intended to be used. Which is shooting, even if it is a paper target in a shooting range. For example, if I spend a couple thousand dollars on a guitar it is because I intend to play that instrument. Having it just living in its case for an eternity does not do it much good. Unless my intent was only to have it as a collectible and plan on reselling it later.

But the question remains, wouldn't I want to at least play it and know how it sounds and feels? Or even find if it works at all? I know I would. That is one of the reasons why I collect guitars – because I enjoy the different tones and feel of each instrument. Making music and playing the instrument is the intended purpose for which it was designed even if I do not decide to go gigging and taking it on the road to mitigate any damage to it. Then again, some instruments become more valuable if they have a "story" rather than just being on their case for however long.

And for most people, I am sure they would do something similar, no matter what purchase they made. The question is still – what is the intended purpose for this purchase? For example, if you are an art collector of sorts and buy an original painting by an artist you admire. It is highly likely that the painting will be displayed somewhere. It will not just be hidden in a basement somewhere out of view. Why? Because art is intended to be displayed and appreciated by different beholders.

But I really want you to keep thinking about the intended purpose for design, as you pair this with critical thinking on otherwise artificial and controversially charged topics. This can even go extended to any mundane objects we purchase. A blender, a coffee maker, a toaster oven, a garage door, a book, a hammer, a bottle opener, a fishing rod, etc. And yes, those objects have been also instrumental in getting somebody killed – either intentionally or partially, or not partially by accident, as contributing factors. The case being when somebody gets electrocuted by an appliance; or even violent rhetoric inspired by a book. Even if the latter was unintentional – hence not designed to take out a life – in either case, it will require <u>human intervention</u> at some point.

As far as weaponizing inventions, it is as old as the time when people roamed the planet. Even in bible allegories you can read

Cain whacking his brother Abel with a weapon furnished from a dead animal. That is in the very first pages of the book of Genesis. Therefore, weaponizing something is not something new. Throughout history, we have seen examples of horrible torture methods. Hence, the innovation to end a life was not only transactional in the end state of killing somebody; but rather in dehumanizing and inflicting as much punishing damage and pain to the victim as possible. This is unfortunately a very real human trait.

For so-called civilized societies, we have elevated ourselves from the savagery we read in history books. But it has not been eliminated. I mentioned earlier that we live in a time where unlimited knowledge is at our fingertips, yet the willful ignorance continues to run rampant. I cannot be kind about it because it is extremely frustrating. Why? Because it is exploitable, and some who learned these perverse tactics are bound to use them and are even walking us back into a dark cycle of our history that was supposed to be surpassed by now.

Unfortunately, history does repeat itself – and it has been repeating itself through the ages. Technology has grown better but there are still a few ideologies which are adamantly keeping us stuck in the back corner. The very same people will be adept to accept very new technology in order to maximize the punishment to their perceived enemies, and yet they would stubbornly cling to bronze era texts. And no, I am not just talking about the bible. There are plenty of other bronze era texts out there.

Why do I keep returning to ideological conversations? Because they are linked, as I mentioned before, to the rhetoric's goal which is to turn the narrative into action. But the idea needs to take traction and find a mind that will be willing to carry said rhetoric into action. Usually, for this to work a person or group with some implied authority will latch to a preconceived notion that could influence somebody. Even if these followers were not pursuing a potentially divisive rhetoric. In either case, we must be aware of the fact that somebody would influence and even prostitute those thoughts into decisions. What thoughts? Whatever thoughts that might have already existed in the follower, or the thoughts that were somehow implanted into the follower by this influencer.

In other words, it creates a need. Much like in marketing, there might be something presented to you that you might have no idea existed before and is trying to answer a question or even solve a problem that you might not have even realized you had. For example, in an infomercial a salesperson will present you with a product that seems to solve a situation, carry out a task, provide convenience, etc. If it is something you can identify as useful, then you will likely buy it. Even if this purchase was impulse buying. It might even cause some buyers' remorse. When it comes to propaganda, it is very similar but a lot more complex on the ultimate intent.

We mentioned this example of propaganda techniques in a previous chapter. The difference between somebody trying to sell you something, and with propaganda, is that there will likely be somebody excluded. There will be an "us against them" narrative and [limited] context. A perceived enemy is introduced, and the divisive narrative starts to infiltrate the minds of their followers. Give it enough time and these seemingly simple disagreements could turn into a time bomb. Especially if the echo chamber continues to discredit the perceived enemy.

With that said, we must understand that this does not mean that we must automatically agree or disagree with either the person who is pushing the narrative or the perceived enemy. What this means is that we must be pragmatically objective. This is different from being an unjustified counter pointer for the sake of rampant skepticism. Being a cynical skeptic and an actual non-naïve person are very different dichotomies. The former being an actual gold mine for a propagandist, and the other a very exploitable source of useful fools. And these people are a lot easier to exploit because they already think they know everything there is to know about a particular topic. Especially if this is a topic, they have gained some interest and perhaps seem to have invested enough level of knowledge to self- proclaim themselves as experts. But that is where it can get dangerous – for all those involved.

Conversely, an actual non-naïve person will also hear the dissenting opinions and narratives. If they have questions or find these counter narratives conflict with their pre-conceived notions, they will make a contentious decision to understand the actual truth. In the search for actual truth there might be some "traps" along the way. These traps are also exploitable, that is possibly already factored into the propagandist's narrative. In other words, it's not just causes and effects, but there will be a sizable gradient of possibilities that are carefully calculated to give the *perception* of an epiphany.

I made that last sentence very long on purpose. Propaganda can range from very direct to very indirect. And it is the indirect type where anything hiding in plain sight gets missed by the follower. But somehow – subconsciously – these seeds take root and are easily harvested by the propagandists when they feel the time is right. It is a subtle brainwashing, and it works.

That is why a lot of the people who happen to become useful fools do not see it coming. They might even feel extremely offended and display a sense of rightful indignation if somebody points to them that they have been swaying victims of a potential narrative. But remember what I said before, everybody has the potential to be a good person, or to sink into the depths of being a terrible human being. It is part of the environment, the level of indoctrination, and the normalization that has become part of the very fabric percolated by their immediate society.

For example, I am personally opposed to any Fascistic ideology pushed by Mussolini, or conversely a Communist ideology pushed by Marxism. To me those are tremendously dangerous extremes. But that does not mean that I have not actually studied them, and I understand their doctrines and principles, in fact. Understanding and knowing those doctrines does not mean that they are going to convince me to be an obedient follower of either one. Why? Because

I have actual intellectual objectivity. If I do not know something I will keep researching – but not only from one source. Otherwise, I will have a much higher probability of falling into circular reasoning. And authoritarians love when circular reasoning is reached by the obedient fools. It just makes it easier to exploit.

However, if you are a reasonable skeptical and have enough introspection to put your notions to the test, then you will have a better chance of gaining objectivity. Especially if you totally dissent from this other source. Does that mean that every single far-fetched opinion out there deserves a second look? Yes, unfortunately, and if relevant to the topic at hand. This relevance might seem tangential, but I know some people who think that they just want the "reader digests" version of events, but that is where the propagandist can implant narratives – or worse – act with impunity. In other words, non-attention to something that could affect you is often taken as tacit consent to push an agenda onto people [people you both care, and do not care about].

Let me give you an illustrative example. Let us say that you are planning on buying a house. But you have no idea about the procedures for buying a home – which is very intricate, by the way. You choose a realtor who happens to be a friend of a friend. Are you good to go with that? Maybe. If this friend of a friend actually teaches you the many facets of home buying – and the anticipated important questions that are relevant to you – to include, but not limited to, the lending options, the escrow, property values, comparable properties in the area, educational districts, access to the highways, proximity to commercial centers, crime rate, if there are any sex offenders within a certain radius, the historical appraisal value of these properties, how safe are the surrounding neighborhoods, are there any plans for any particular industry moving nearby, proximity to waste areas, etc. And we have not even looked inside the house itself. Context and details matter.

So, let us look at the actual property. The actual land where it is sitting. Is it prone to flooding? Does it have any water damage, or mold? How old are the appliances? How well maintained are the machines that are installed within the home? For example, water tanks, air conditioning units, furnaces. Even more basic, what is the condition of the electricity and plumbing? What about the foundation? Is the house sinking or lopsided? Is the crawl space a mess? Are all the faucets working? Are all the lights turning off and on?

Stupid questions, right? Well, no – not if they are damaged and you're going to have to fix that stuff. You'll find out that seemingly simple defects can be very costly if not properly addressed. For example, a leaking toilet or faucet can add up to a lot of money on wasted water which you must pay for, by the way. Or worse, it could be an issue that is leaking outside of any obvious view and the water damage can create all kinds of hidden damage ranging from structural to biohazard concerns. And I am not even scratching the surface on the topic of home buying.

So, this friend of a friend might be able to sit down with you and go over everything and help you find the perfect house. Or this person might get you "a" house while collecting on the commission and move on with their life and forget they ever met you. However, after you sign the many documents to get this house you soon enough start to discover all of the problems that you could and should have addressed before this enormous investment decision.

In other words, did the latter type of person help you? And how much should you have already researched before the decision? Where were any of the biases or red flags that could have been identified? Often, because it is a friend of a friend there is a lot of leeway on what we are willing to risk for the sake of not compromising <u>one</u> factor in the equation – for this example, the relationship that you have with the friend who recommended this other friend to you.

You might be asking yourself how does this example relate to the topic at hand? It is simple – context and attention to detail. We all have blind spots, every one of us. But we do have opportunities to make educated decisions – although it might seem as though a certain decision was made under duress. In the example above, perhaps your friend is really, in fact, concerned about you and the previous person – this "realtor friend?" Maybe they had a good reputation before. Maybe this "realtor friend" just got lucky before and found a good property for somebody else without looking. Or, maybe the "realtor friend" was just trying to get rid of a property and pass it on to the most naïve person they could find and trick them with this bad investment.

Similarly, with a propagandist; there might be people who get into a deal with the best of intentions. But there is somebody with some insider knowledge trying to take leverage over the unsuspecting victims. Or, in some cases, the self-proclaimed leader is not well informed and has blind spots that are also well hidden from view, and these become the blind spots for their followers as well.

If a person gets in a position of authority, but they are not ready to enact that authority by understanding the dynamics of whomever they are trying to lead, then there will be blind spots. If this self-proclaimed leader is an egotistical moron, then they will even refuse to try to learn from these mistakes, let alone even taking valuable advice from others. And that is, by the way, how authoritarians end up losing. They surround themselves by "yes" people so the unescapable fallacies will be condoned even if those fallacies will surely erode that great "empire" that they believed they had forged.

The dangerous part is that while this situation is devolving, an authoritarian will lose all control of the situation with loneliness at the top. Afterall, they cannot let anybody see them as vulnerable. It becomes a self-fulfilling dark prophecy. That is why a lot of authoritarians at the end are paranoid and erratic.

But as they descend into this madness, the followers – especially the most obedient fools – will be tasked with all kinds of extraordinarily sadistic duties, especially if these useful fools were already convinced that their cause was worthy. Even for these useful fools, a violent death would be a perceived vindication for their misguided actions. That is what I was telling you before. The authoritarian is only as strong as his or her followers.

If you expected to hear some authoritarian sadistic porn, this is not the chapter for that. The warning at the top of this chapter is generalized, as it is meant to bring introspection. That's the real lesson for this chapter and these introspections can be harder for some more than for others. With that being said, there are plenty of examples of incredibly sadistic inflictions of pain onto perceived enemies out there. These atrocities have occurred from the beginning of civilization, and even in the pre-historic past. If you are looking for that type of violent content, you are sure to find plenty of that almost everywhere. My intent is to help you think critically and to avoid becoming an authoritarians' useful fool. Useful fools consistently find themselves on the wrong side of history, even if centuries go by.

CHAPTER 9

TRUE VICTORY |
The Adversary is Only as Powerful as his Followers

*The more I see it, the more it becomes evident – people can be exponentially naïve. You, me, everybody – we are all people, and we can all be naïve about something, or someone. If you have not experienced this in your life, you are either a mythical creature or somebody is gaslighting you right now and you have not realized it yet. And this is important to realize because we all could be confused about something based on our biases and our ability to selectively enact blind trust. This blind trust can grow if there are factors that incite you to confirm your justification for this blind trust. It can be indoctrination, it can be infatuation, or it can be professional admiration. Hey, it can even be actual true love for somebody who has gained our high esteem. Much like that first love. You know that boyfriend/girlfriend we thought was a love that would last forever, but now it is one of our exes.
This concept applies to everything in life.*

I have spoken about biases in his book extensively, there is a big reason for that. A bias is exploitable and can control us. These biases can make something unappealing look fascinating, or even coveting this "something" as something we consider to be part of our very fabric. It could be any random interest that turns into an obsession. Paradoxically enough, some of these could be beneficial for us, and of course become defining factors in our life. That is why it can be so easy for a propagandist to create a need that will turn obsessive enough. Again, turning rhetoric into action.

And it is obviously in the action where the end state of the rhetoric can get measured as effective or ineffective. For a parallel comparison: Is something trendy or not? Or is it fashionable or not? Events, people, fashion, trends, technology, fads, memes, these can be all the rage for a while and fall out of favor at some other point. For example, even a very beautifully decorated home in a movie might seem very dated once a few decades go by. Even if you lived in that decade, looking back at those days – it could feature a look [such as fashion] you might or might not want to recreate. It will depend on how your taste has evolved over the years.

Let me give you another example, have you recently watched a movie or TV show you used to love? Do you still love it now? Or maybe it just feels different in a negative way? Perhaps you still enjoy it, but it's just not the same as before? If you feel that way, this is normal and expected. These feelings will range from nostalgia to "don't like it anymore" – it will occur and manifest depending on many factors. For example, perhaps that movie you used to enjoy now has what it would be considered an "outdated reference" that was socially acceptable and condoned back then, but today would make you cringe.

It can also be the other way around. Maybe there was something that made you cringe – or a reference that went way above your head back in the day. But now, as you have learned more context these references make sense. I remember when I was a kid and watched a funny movie. I might have even laughed a lot. But then as I grew up and saw it again, and learned more about something that was perhaps contemporary when the movie was released, then I was able to enjoy this movie even more – often because these otherwise obscure references I missed were now noticeably clear.

And there is a reason why I bring this example. When we are still in the learning phases of a topic, or maybe did not gain enough experience to juxtapose other competing relevant topics – we might unwittingly suffer from a tunnel vision scenario. The little bit of knowledge we get will seem as though it was already a lot of information. You would likely feel like you have mastered a topic. This is in fact a logical fallacy. It is part of the Dunning-Kruger effect.

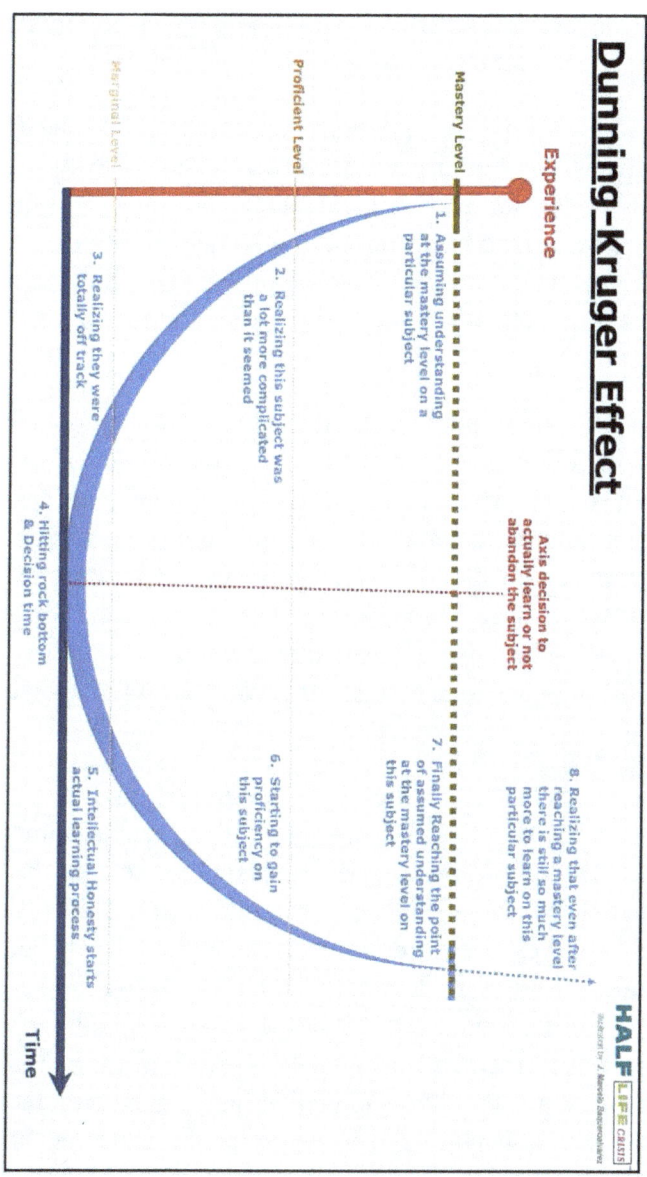

Here is this graphic referenced again. As I said before in this book, I also spoke extensively about this Dunning-Kruger Effect in my other books. But to make it easier for us all, that is why I am putting the same graphic you saw earlier in this book once again in this chapter. I have a feeling it will make more sense now that we have covered a lot more context.

But in the meantime, let us recap. The premise for the Dunning-Kruger Effect is when a person knows extraordinarily little about something and somehow erroneously assumes he/she knows everything there is to know about *that* something. But it is not until they undergo the exhaustive learning process that they realize there is so much more to learn, even after arriving to the so-called mastery level of knowledge.

When it comes to authoritarians, they thrive when people they want as obedient followers get stuck in this assumption of knowledge. It is even better when these obedient followers are narcissistic themselves. Some are even very pedantic about pushing a de facto false narrative. And some of these people would do that because they believe in some circular reasoning, flawed document, or argument for authority. They erroneously assume that this fallacy already answers all the questions that an otherwise pragmatic person would challenge.

And notice that I used the term pragmatic and not skeptical. There are some skeptics that are <u>way off</u> on their assumption. For example, there are skeptical people out there asserting the fact that this planet where we all live is not actually round. Yes, the planet is round. And yes, we used a similar example earlier, because the fact remains. And their skepticism is based on pseudo-science and incorrect information. However, they are very adamant about trying to confirm this incorrect information. And if they find enough people who share the same logical fallacy, they will likely cling to that erroneous narrative. The way out of a false narrative is by understanding dissenting opinions and deciding if these opinions are based on facts.

Also, for a fact to be such it needs to be logical, measurable, and demonstrable. The burden of proof is always on the person making the claim. If I erroneously claim that I had an out-of- body experience where I turned into a seagull and flew around the world in 12 seconds five times – that is a very bold claim. Can I prove that *that* happens? Absolutely not.

Some other claims are a bit harder to show because they are unfalsifiable. That means that I cannot prove whether that happened or not within an actual scientific method. And scientific methods can be either concrete or abstract – yet measurable. For example, mathematical calculations. In some instances, such as in calculus, the numbers tend to be gigantic, and nobody would be able to physically count every number individually. But by calculating with this proven method, you can process exceptionally large numbers effectively.

If a claim is unfalsifiable, then it would not be something you can prove. For example, if I would be to claim that there is a planet in the opposite side of the Milky Way galaxy that is known by their inhabitants as A-440 and it is ruled by a deity who punishes apostates by lashing them with a guitar string, it might sound ridiculous. But can you prove such a planet does not in fact exist? With our current technology we cannot.

But the next logical question would be, "how do you know?" Did I have an epiphany? Or maybe did I observe it through a telescope? One of those would be a more obvious lie than the other. Which one? The second claim. We do not have a telescope that is potent enough to view that far into the other side of the galaxy with that level of resolution. Also, even if we could, the other side of the galaxy is so many light years away that it would be like looking several thousand years into the past of said planet (our galaxy is about 100,000 light years across). In other words, the light of those images could take thousands of years to reach the telescope lenses.

With the first claim – still it is unfalsifiable – but harder to prove. For example, there are literally thousands of religions. Some made up of and by people which legitimately believe in their doctrines and some other *religions* which were intentionally created as satire. Yet they are all legal religions. For example, there is a religion which has Satan as the central deity, but it is in fact an atheistic satirical religion. Atheists do not believe in any god, and that also means they do not believe in any devil either. This made up "religion" is more about introspection and the "self" [which is different from selfish]. However, there are a lot of theistic people who are terrified of their *rituals*, because their erroneously assumed secondhand interpretations of this made-up religion. For example, they assume they do all kinds of demonic things as depicted in *their own* religious allegories.

But these feelings and assumptions can also be a lot further from religion. It can really apply to any human emotion that can draw intent towards a person or a group of people. For example, how many times have you had a crush on somebody, even if you knew that such a relationship was never going to come to fruition? However, this human factor could create a visceral response bias towards this person in particular. Maybe this crush turned out to be a heart-breaking situation, and suddenly this person for whom you held such high esteem is now an example of deception and someone you do not want to see any more for as long as you breathe on this planet. But maybe, you might find the same person years later when the circumstances are different. Perhaps now you will see those idiosyncrasies as menial, or perhaps even as justifiable. On the other side of the spectrum, you might be able to confirm if your gut feeling about this person when your heart was broken was indeed based on facts.

All this illustrates that people are complex and that we all can have certain juncture points that make us remarkably like one another.

For some of you too young to remember there was a social media site called "Myspace" before Facebook took over. Myspace was an immensely popular site, and around the same time there was this other social media platform called "Hi-5." You might have heard about Myspace; many people likely have no idea about Hi-5. Yet, they had some following, but they were unable to keep up with Facebook which started even later than Hi-5. Little by little Hi-5 and MySpace were not the "cool sites to have." All the buzz was moving towards Facebook. Then Facebook became what it is today. Of course, along the way Facebook continued improving and reinventing itself until it became as familiar as what you have seen today [at the time I write this manuscript]. Even though you can argue they have made a lot of mistakes along the way. Regardless, it was the <u>people</u> who made Facebook what it is now. Also, it was the lack of people what made MySpace and Hi-5 shrivel and relegate to a relic of the virtual past. Despite all of them being similar in principle and technology at the time.

You might still be able to log in to those old sites, but they are nowhere near as big as Facebook. Fast forward and Facebook also have a lot of prominent social media competitors. But I will leave it at that because I could write an entire book about social media competition. Moving on.

Followers, people, and their attention are what can fuel a movement, a brand, or even an authoritarian. We spoke in an earlier chapter; Hitler's party was considered a radical fringe movement before they gained some political acumen and rose to power. In fact, this party almost disappeared when they got arrested early in their history. But then after regrouping they learned about their mistakes and were able to capitalize on otherwise good principles – such as patriotism and prostitute those principles to push a false rhetoric. These doctrines were then peppered with a few cherry-picked facts to give a sense of legitimization. But again, remember that they skewed the context on purpose.

As the people started to manifest that visceral feeling, then an enemy – a scapegoat, a sacrificial lamb was needed to direct that newfound fury. And sparking this fury was not an extremely hard task. People throughout history have been frustrated about something or someone in their environment. Usually whomever is in charge of making decisions at the time of discontent. Then somebody who <u>poses</u> as a *viable* solution for change comes around. But the change occurs for the worse. The rhetoric was inciting action that would only be beneficial to the very top of *that* food chain.

We spoke about this before in this book. An authoritarian can fly just so high before their wings are cutoff and fall from grace. And usually this is a self-induced wound. The authoritarian will tend to come full circle, and some have even found a violent end. Especially if they collected a lot of enemies along the way. People who have been wronged, especially if they are subjugated and brutalized, tend not to be so kind towards their wrongdoers when the power roles reverse.

For example, how many times have you heard in modern history about a western nation where a politician who comes from the fringes starts some sort of divisive rhetoric? If said political figure has not gained enough momentum [and followers], the other candidates will point out every flaw and raise every red flag possible on their rhetoric. But what about if this radicalized politician gets enough traction? You might see the same dissenting figures after rallying behind this otherwise divisive person. In fact, they might go as far as to justify, gaslight, or otherwise condone this divisive person's antics. Meanwhile, everybody else who was not persuaded by this person will be pointing out the obvious about this divisive rhetoric. They might even point out the hypocrisy of those who rightfully attacked this divisive person's rhetoric and then suddenly changed their tune.

But if the divisive figure falls from grace, then the very same hypocritical people who were condoning the divisive person antics will likely disavow him/her. And surprise-surprise, joins the correct impression from everybody else who did not buy into that divisive rhetoric. Which was [likely] by the way the same rhetoric they were attacking when this divisive person showed up from the fringes in the first place.

In other words, when it comes to authoritarianism some people realized from the get-go that this figure, personality, or political movement was bad news. And as time will move forward these pragmatic skeptics will be proven right about their disdain for this divisive figure.

Authoritarians are divisive, even though they would unify seemingly like-minded individuals. Some of these individuals might be pursuing a false narrative. In many instances this narrative will be taking the form of misguided patriotism. Also, a lot of the people vulnerable to a divisive person tend to be people of faith. Any faith. Through the thousand years humanity has been roaming the planet, there was usually some regard for some sort of "higher power." Sometimes that power was a deity, sometimes the power was the state, sometimes the deity was a person who became a representation of a state.

This predisposition to blindly follow [a] faith opens the door to deception. And I know some people might feel offended about this. They would think – "Well, that does not happen with MY faith! Because MY faith is the one and only true one." Sure, to you… and maybe to those close to your circle. But for others outside this paradigm, THEIR faith and <u>only</u> THEIR faith is the only <u>true</u> one. And your faith to them is – let us say, a fantasy. Do you feel the same way about theirs? [<u>Their</u> faith] Even if you respect their right to worship whatever they want to worship? What if they worship the sun? What if they worship butterflies? What if they worship Satan? What if they worship a volcano? Those feelings of devotion are just as real to them as yours are to you.

That is why it is so important to gain as much intellectual honesty as possible. Challenge your own beliefs and find the actual sources that are unbiased and objectively peer reviewed. The truth is somewhere in the middle. Remember that extraordinary claims require extraordinary proof. Science in general, all the different actual sciences give methods to find the closest approximation to empirical truth. Science is always trying to disprove itself to ensure we have not missed something along the way, or worse… for instance, ensuring we have not fallen victims of circular reasoning.

Some people erroneously say that they do not believe in science. But that is not how it works. Science is not a matter of belief; it is a matter of whether you understand it or not. In order to ascend to a <u>theory</u>, which in science is the highest level of the scientific process. It means that it has been tested repeatedly with different methods and they yielded the same conclusion. These methods are measurable and demonstrable. Again, as I mentioned there are measurable methods that transcend what we can see and perceive with our limited senses. But these methods can be accurately enacted.

For example, when we landed on the moon, or on Mars, or on Venus, or even send spaceships to other planets and moons in our solar system. We cannot measure with a physical ruler the distances. But we know how to find those distances by other means that are proven to be exactly accurate. That is of course a lot more complex than what I am willing to type in this book because those are extensive subjects in their own right. But the point to all this is that there is a process. There are smart people behind that process. And for these people it might have been their lives' work to toil on one little part of the gigantic puzzle that adds to the reality we can collectively enjoy.

When it comes to following somebody who claims to hold the "truth," we have two choices. Follow the right path or follow the ramblings of a charlatan who is in it for himself or herself. The right path is the one that helps everybody have a better life. The path that is not divisive, but rather that helps us work together. Authoritarians hate that because they need conflict to galvanize their power. This conflict might be intrinsic or extrinsic to their own environment, but they need that in order to pose themselves as the only viable "solution" to the problem.

In reality, you might disagree with me. You might think: "There is no actual problem. It is all manufactured, it is made believe." But then again, this manufactured problem has become a tangible reality to so many. It is in-fact somebody's drama that had gone haywire.

And the drama becomes powerful because the people involved give it enough attention to make it a problem. Let me give you another illustrative example.

In the movie Whiplash (spoiler alert – if you haven't watched it yet, skip to next page), the main character wants to be a jazz drummer. He is adamant about pursuing this passion. His teacher can be seen by many as an authoritarian weird man who runs a very prestigious music program in the university where the main character attends. This teacher is an abusive person, yet this young musician would take all this abuse because he wanted to be that phenomenal jazz musician. The abusive teacher would cloak his methods as a motivation for bringing that *strong* spirit from within his students. In the end the young drummer became a phenomenal player, even though the teacher by then got fired for his crazy antics. If you have not yet seen it, you should watch the movie Whiplash. It is a great movie, and a lot more intricate than what I just mentioned. Yes, even with the spoilers I mentioned, there is still plenty more to discover.

The point being that if a person has a particular predisposition and passion, they will go as far as their sprit will take them despite any obstacles along the way. An authoritarian figure can find these spirited people and prostitute their motivation to turn them into obedient useful fools. The muscle behind their agenda. But remember, even that muscle is a disposable commodity for the authoritarian. In the end the authoritarian is only looking for one person alone. Himself or herself.

So why should we be given any authoritarian power? Simple answer, we <u>should not</u> give the authoritarian any power. They cannot responsibly use it. If you seek more complexity in that answer, it is because the decision of who we consider adequate for our enjoying devotion is within each one of us, but the result will affect us collectively for better or worse. Depending on whether we let somebody run our lives with impunity. Apathy, and willful ignorance will just make the authoritarians' process much easier to rise to power. Why? Because it becomes a mathematical situation.

Let us say that in a group of 100 people there is one who wants to be the authoritarian leader. There are 40 people who really want this person to be in power for whatever reason – justified or not, they just like the guy. And there are 35 who can really see the problem ahead and are opposed about this person gaining any more power. And there are 25 people who do not participate in the decision, either because they do not pay attention, or they do not care, or they are just not informed, so they won't decide one way or the other. Then the 40 people who really want this authoritarian guy (including himself) to be in charge just made the decision for the remainder of 60 people.

As predicted this team of 100 people is now an authoritarian nightmare, but now they are all stuck with this authoritarian figure. It would have only taken six people from the willful ignorant to pay more attention and perhaps mitigated this problem from existing in the first place… should a vote be taken. Now, turn these numbers into percentages, and you will find something closer to reality. The numbers will change for and against the authoritarian wannabe, but what still is constant is a significant percentage of people not paying attention, therefore becoming tacit consent for those who end up deciding on their behalf. Good or bad.

With this context, as we reach the end of this book, my commitment to you is to give you the information in this book as a way to open our minds. Be able to think outside the box. And when we are skeptical about something, ensure that we are not just being cynical morons who are in fact following the script of an authoritarian. There are plenty of useful fools out there. We all might have fallen into that category at some point in our lives. If you have, do not feel bad. It is not how we fall, but rather how we recover that ultimately makes the difference.

Look inside your train of thought, find the red flags. Compare the rhetoric that is being fed to you by all those who "agree with you" and juxtapose those narratives with dissenting rhetoric. The truth is somewhere in the middle. I just caution you, do not just breeze through it. There is an inherited level of complexity even on simple things. In fact, if it is too simple – there might be something else to the story that is out of sight. That does not mean that it is intrinsically nefarious. But as I mentioned to you, even when it comes to objects that can kill – those are not necessarily designed to end a person. People have been killed with a butter knife or a screwdriver... but that is not what those instruments were designed for. And the same is true for rhetoric – they might be presenting it as something different to the audience – but there could be an intent behind it, something that ends up hidden in the seemingly simplified façade.

Hindsight is always 20/20, but how many times have you done something wrong and wished you could have gone back in time to fix it? We cannot change the past, but we can forge a better future for us all. Together.

Just as the authoritarian is only as strong as the followers he or she has on their corner; so, can a good cause destined to create a better future for us all. It is our choice. What do we want it to be? Do we want to be somebody's useful fool? Or do we want to be a contributor to make a better world?

I will give you two examples of stuff that have made it better for us. Science and technology. Science is something all educated people, no matter where they come from, can agree on. We have scientist from every corner of the world... they can agree as they experiment on the hypothesis until they can have enough evidence to ascend it to a theory. Then if this theory is valid and irrefutable then ascents to what is known as a law. This takes time and collective effort. Trial and error, and most importantly intellectual honesty to ensure we all benefit from these advances. For example, the very media where you are reading this book is due to the evolution of technological advances. A team effort!

There is so much science involved in this very interaction we are having as you read my words. Decades and even centuries of knowledge both in technology and cultural sciences came together for me to type this manuscript with this tablet. Somebody before me came up with a keyboard idea, and right now through experimentation and technological evolution it has improved to the point I am able to effortlessly pass my ideas onto you. It does not end up there, there is a gigantic cadre of computer science programmers who put the software together on the first iteration of concept. And now several versions after I can type and pre-audit my book in the font I prefer, while sitting alone in the Mess Hall onboard USS COLE (where I am typing this book).

Some people might dislike science and demonize it. But guess what? They receive help from it every day. Have you taken a hot shower today? Science. Got a nice cup of coffee with your Keurig machine? Science. Got to drive your automobile through the roads and make it to work? Science, science, science. The products of science are all around us. Your cell phone technology for example. There were many different sciences working together to make that happen. That roof over your head? Many scientists came together to ensure it is not going to cave in, that it is not going to leak, that it is not going to collapse, that it is going to keep the temperature in check inside the home. Science. When people demonize science, they are in fact renouncing their own best interests.

I find it funny, for example people going on social media talking bad about science when the fact they can do that misguided comment is also thanks to science. And not only <u>one</u> science but sciences <u>collaborating</u> in unison. That understanding of reality is one influencing factor we should all be following – even if you are not a scientist. We can all become a part of the solution. You will find out that there is a lot more that makes us similar than what makes us different. The more you learn, the more you realize that there is a great complex world out there.

Sure, people have different cultures and customs, but they all can be fascinating and work in harmony. In the great scheme of things, the things that divide us – even the strategic geopolitical level are in fact very trivial. Yet there are some sensitivities that make these disagreements more complex than they should.

And I go back to this, religion is one of those sensitivities. Politics is another. However, these two are very much intermixed. I have advocated for it before, a grown-up conversation about politics and religion is way overdue – but for this conversation to happen, the introspective dialog [as in seeing more than one point of view objectively] first needs to happen within <u>yourself</u>. There is a reason why a lot of religions put the very thought of being objective over their own faith as a blasphemous sin. But it is not. If you are immensely proud of your faith, would you not want to know everything about it?

And more importantly how it came to be? But most importantly being able to PROVE that it is true with empirical <u>facts</u> and not faith alone? How many other religious rituals and doctrines might have a similar story to your faith? And more importantly what makes your own religion the only true one? Not because that is what your religious leader says, but because you can independently understand the differences between <u>every</u> faith out there. Trust me, it will change your life – for the best, if you are objective and intellectually honest.

When you see the world from an elevated perspective, you will realize that most of our quarrels are petty. However, they have been given a very extrinsically aggregated value, based on whatever our societal norms dictate. And yes, sometimes that means that we must conform to certain guidelines that form part of the social structure we have been put upon. However, that societal sanctioned normalization does not always align with reality about right from wrong when it comes to empirical facts and actions.

I will give you an example, as I type this manuscript, I am active duty in the U.S. Navy. I am very much reaching the end of my military career as I near my retirement date. There are many norms, and rules and with those rules restrictions we must abide while in uniform. However, once my active service is up and I retire these same imposed rigors become the past. My wife retired earlier this year [when I typed this manuscript] from the U.S. Navy as well. Now she has the freedom to paint her nails anyway she wishes. There are no longer any drills or other constraining requirements she must follow while in uniform. Her decisions are her own – yet this freedom does not mean she is reckless. She makes decisions that are beneficial to our family, as well as for herself. Meanwhile, while I am in service – today – for example as I type this, I am on duty on a Friday night. It is just 15 minutes before taps (2200 – time to go to bed), and I must spend the night away from my family onboard this ship. Even though the ship is moored right now literally less than a 15 minutes' drive away from my house. Yet, I cannot make the decision on my own to leave this ship and stay home with my wife and daughter.

But being in the Navy was a voluntary decision. This is what I expected I would have to do. And I will do that, until my time – like my wife's time in uniform ends. You see, the decision we make do not mean that we are stuck with them forever… at least not in every case. Sometimes we cannot take back things we did in the past.

But generally speaking, a lot of decisions we make, even if some end up being mistakes, can be recovered and later become the catalyst to a better solution. It is part of a process. Things evolve, procedures evolve, and yes creatures – even us humans evolve. We are constantly evolving – that is why you will not see a "hard transitional fossil" – it is because the changes are gradual, and they will continue to adapt and morph to different environments. Something similar happened to our experiences. It is a gradient, not a swatch pallet.

Most of the time our minds will be adapting and evolving little by little. Unless there is an event that will rock our world for better or worse and will accelerate this process. But you see, we can do that because we have the power of reasoning and assessing our environment.

There are too many charlatans out there. They will let you know that everything is easily resolved as long as <u>they</u> alone (or their group of cronies) are the solution to that situation (whatever it is that they advocate for). Even if it is complicated – they will assert that only <u>they</u> hold the key to make it better. I submit to you that we are <u>all</u> learning. We all have blind spots, but we can help each other collectively to become better. What decision will you make for your life and the lives of those around you? Our future is forged every day by our individual and collective actions. Thank you for reading my book! HLC

ACKNOWLEDGEMENT

THANK YOU! First, to all my readers, I appreciate you so much for taking the time to read my words. I realize you could be reading or doing anything else, and you chose to read what I had to say. I value that very much!

Thank you to my wife, Alicia, and my daughter, Samantha, for always being there for me, even if I am on the opposite side of the planet from time to time– just like the very moment I started typing this book. Love has no bounds, and I love you both no matter if you are in my arms or halfway around the world. I love you all the same, but I wish I were closer (especially as I write this). Fortunately, as I am typing this paragraph the ship is in homeport so I am not extremely far from my girls, and I can go to sleep at home a lot more often than before.

Thank you to the crew of the USS COLE (DDG 67) during this historic deployment (as well as my final) to the Fifth and Sixth Fleets Areas of Operations. We have shared a lot of memorable moments during this deployment, and so many adventures. Afterall, we were literally in the same boat for so many months! I love all of you, but I am happy that by the time I finished this manuscript I was off the boat and spending time with my girls.

My gratitude to whomever it is that will end up publishing and distributing this book– which at the time I am writing this, I have no idea who it will be…not yet anyway. I might arrange things solo with an outlet I have not yet decided on, or a self-publishing company as an e-book, audio book, or who knows? Once I know I will add the proper credit to the *publishing and admin rights* page (Yes, I am keeping this paragraph because it's definitely happening–let's live with it). And yes, you might see this same line in all of my books because it stays true.

EPILOGUE

The manuscript for

AUTHORITARIANISM & PROPAGANDA
| The Puppet Master Tools

is finally a tangible reality!

This is the third book manuscript I started writing during this deployment. I started writing this manuscript on Wednesday, August 31, 2022, and I finished writing the last chapter yesterday, Friday, December 2, 2022. The proof- reading process is probably going to take a while, and as lengthy as the time it took to write this book. A few important life events occurred since I started the manuscript, so I am glad I waited. As a result, my knowledge continued to grow and – in the process – helped to advance the book.

With that being said, I will be very busy again in the near future and the pace of the publishing process will be based on that. I predict it will take a few, or rather several months, so it is what it is. So, I am going to do my best to speed up the process as much as possible because this topic is emergently relevant.

One of these factors is the growth of knowledge based on real- world events. There is plenty to speak about on the topic of contemporary geopolitical situations around the world. As I emphasized over and over in this book, I will not be talking about any contemporary or current authoritarian regime – not calling them by name, and rather only cite historical figures in this book.

The purpose of my book was to provide context and afford the reader an opportunity to spark their curiosity to learn more on their own. Hopefully, this will give them an idea of how the information they will potentially encounter will be laid out and, more importantly, if there are any false narratives that might confuse their path along the way.

The intent of my book was to only scratch the surface. That is why the book is relatively short in comparison to my other books, and one of the reasons why I wanted to make it shorter. Because of the urgency of the world situation, it's not just important where we are today but where we are heading tomorrow.

Ultimately, I want a safer world, one where my daughter will grow and thrive. It might feel a bit self-serving but the way I see it, my daughter came into the world from me and my wife so therefore *I* am directly responsible for affording her the best opportunity to blossom. Part of that means giving her the tools to become the person she is meant to be and – while she is learning – I am doing my part in making sure her world will be a better place.

It is startling to me that the more I talk with some of my contemporaneous fellow men and women at this point in time, the less informed they seem to be about the realities of where the world is heading. Even more disturbing, those people are very aware of the fact the world continues to deteriorate under the looming threat of authoritarianism, but they feel that it is "somebody else's" concern, not theirs. News flash, this problem would affect us all, even if we think we are not in a place where authoritarianism and propaganda prevail. These two factors have been alive and well for a long time, and that is why it seems almost analogous to the rest of our societal structure. Fortunately, there are others in the new generation who are a lot more receptive to understanding these intricacies. Afterall, they will inherit this world.

After having conversations with people growing up in this new era, fortunately they seem to be willing to be part of the solution. The solution is simple, but I cannot rely on only one person, but it does start with one, and that's us.

This is the solution: Control what you own, even if it is only a little bit at the time. By controlling what you own, you will learn how you enact critical thinking development. Change yourself for the better (as we all have room for improvement) and this will, in turn, create a culture of positive change around you. Just know that it takes some time, sometimes requiring longer times to see a significant improvement depending on how entranced your societal environment has become to a particular narrative ruling the land.

In either case, there is no monument for those who left things as they were. To make a positive change, it does not necessarily need a revolution, but it does need intellectual curiosity to find areas for improvement, and to then improve upon those findings.

I realize that some might find my words idealistic, but they are not. I would rather qualify them as an omen, and even a warning for what could happen next. Somebody who is more curious than the willfully ignorant would rather take over an uninformed person's lives, followed by tacit consent, because ignorance tends to choose to bury its head in the sand while the adversary rules in de facto over their destiny.

Things have not gotten any better, and authoritarian minions are planting rhetorical seeds in all corners of the world. You do not need to go too far to find instances for this reality. This is likely going to be my first book release among all of my manuscripts I have written during this deployment as the others will be released afterward to give additional context and expand the lessons included herein.

I will end on a positive note. You and I, and everybody in our lives are the future of this world. We can make it better if we choose to do so. We do not need to take arms; we just need to ensure we galvanize our support against whatever will stunt growth and peace. Together, we can drive fringe destructive ideas back to the fringes. Then those destructive concepts will have a natural demise because they will not find fertile ground for blind followers. The future is what we make of it. The more proactive we are, the more control we have over our destiny.

ABOUT THE BOOK

Authoritarianism and Propaganda come hand in hand. They have been related from the very start. An authoritarian is only as powerful as their followers. Are you being bamboozled into being a useful fool for an authoritarian? Let us find out together. In this book, we will get to speak about all of those important factors that give an authoritarian leverage over our own lives and our very futures. And make no mistake – a useful fool is disposable in the view of the authoritarian. The only person an authoritarian cares about is himself or herself. Authoritarianism can vary in size and scope. It can be as monumental as a world leader, or as minimal as a family unit. Yes, a micro version of the same monster. The archnemesis against an authoritarian and their propagandists are pragmatic, think critically, and use intellectual honesty. Within these pages, we will discuss how you can stay ahead of authoritarian rhetoric. The authoritarian and propagandists want to turn this rhetoric into action, and these actions do not have your best interests in mind even if you are fighting on their side, so it's crucial to learn about the facts that are hidden in plain sight. Are you ready to open your mind?

ABOUT THE AUTHOR

J. Marcelo Baqueroalvarez was born in San Francisco de Quito, Republic of Ecuador. After moving to the United States in 1995, he enrolled and graduated Fort Lauderdale High School and subsequently college at the Art Institute of Fort Lauderdale with Magna Cum Laude in 1999. Simultaneously, he worked in video production and multimedia with his family until 2003 when he enlisted in the United States Navy. During his tenure in uniform, he traveled the world and was stationed at several commands, including USS SEATTLE (AOE-3), USS LAKE ERIE (CG-70), USS ABRAHAM LINCOLN (CVN-72), USS COLE (DDG-67) and additional commands on shore and overseas. He rose to the rank of Senior Chief Petty Officer. During his time in the Navy, he met his wife, Alicia, and they welcomed to the world their daughter, Samantha. Marcelo is an avid lover of the arts, particularly in music, graphic art, photography, videography, and writing. He uses his unique leadership style to nurture his peers, subordinates, and seniors, hoping to inspire and bring team cohesion. In 2013, he founded BeeZee Vision, LLC™ as an opportunity to expand his artistic acumen. He also started the Half Life Crisis™ project where he shares his unique points of view for posterity, doing what he loves doing the most which is stating facts.

ABOUT HALF LIFE CRISIS™

Half Life Crisis™ is the brainchild of J. Marcelo "BeeZee" Baqueroalvarez.

The simple concept is complex in execution. Half Life Crisis™ is not synonym with "midlife crisis." Half Life Crisis™ is the fact that we spend most of our lives making a living rather than living our lives. The project was designed as a catalyst to give his creator an avenue to do what he loves most. Which is to "rant," a lot, about all kinds of things he finds interesting or fascinating. During these "rants" he tells facts with exuberant detail. He has his say via the many media manifestations under the Half Life Crisis™ construct. Afterall, that is the entire reason Half Life Crisis™ was conceived in the first place. The project is aimed to be of interest to any person who is familiar with the concept of "adulting" – under the pragmatic understanding that not everybody who circled the sun 18 times or more actually qualifies as a functional adult. Half Life Crisis™ celebrates all those who have earned their "adulthood" even if they are under 18 years of age.

Because life is what we make of it...

www.halflifecrisis.com

ABOUT BEEZEE VISION, LLC™

BeeZee Vision, LLC™ was founded on July 15, 2013, in the city of Chesapeake, Virginia, USA by J. Marcelo "BeeZee" Baqueroalvarez. The original idea from BeeZee Vision started in early 2005. BeeZee Vision, LLC™ is the brainchild of J. Marcelo Baqueroalvarez, and the company was founded along with brother David R. Baquero as a web-development and multimedia company in 2003. The company supplies fully customized and automated professional web development services, as well as various selected multimedia services. The name BeeZee Vision comes from Marcelo's U.S. Navy nickname "BeeZee," which derives from his last name Baqueroalvarez, which in Navy jargon it means "Well Done." Creating professional and artistically inspired multimedia projects are Marcelo's personal vision and commitment.

BeeZee Vision, LLC™ serves as the multimedia vehicle for Marcelo's Half Life Crisis™ project. These books are the first iteration of BeeZee Vision, LLC™ embarking in publishing written material from concept to completion.

www.beezeevision.com
www.BZVweb.com

PUBLISHING ADMIN AND RIGHTS

This entire book was written by J. Marcelo Baqueroalvarez. There are no co-authors, though his wife Alicia D. Baqueroalvarez at some point offered to be the preliminary editor. Afterall, English is Marcelo's third language, so one day... sometime... he plans on learning how to speak proper English. Today is not that day, tomorrow does not look good either. There is a non-zero chance Alicia changed her mind, and this book was likely professionally edited at some point. Possibly by Marcelo Baqueroalvarez himself using Artificial Intelligence software. Hey, modern problems require modern solutions, right?

The book was written onboard USS COLE (DDG-67) during the ship's 2021-2022 deployment with the USS HARRY S. TRUMAN (CVN-76) Carrier Strike Group, and circa the time the ships returned to homeport in Norfolk, Virginia.

The entire book's manuscript was typed using his Microsoft Surface Pro tablet/laptop, in Microsoft Word. Seriously, even the layout and fonts were done in the same laptop... on his lap, while he was laying after the workday in his sleeping quarters, or in one of the mess halls onboard the ship.

This book and its contents are the intellectual property of J. Marcelo Baqueroalvarez, and distributed under Half Life Crisis™ and BeeZee Vision, LLC. ™, both also owned by J. Marcelo Baqueroalvarez. The rights of this book extend to his wife Alicia D. Baqueroalvarez and daughter Samantha B. Baqueroalvarez... and that is it. If there are any other publishing houses, then we will talk business then. But this manuscript was typed only by Marcelo.

Alicia and Samantha Baqueroalvarez also own the rights for this book. It will remain so, unless officially noted otherwise. That has not happened yet, the book is likely going to be self-published.

But ideally, we will have follow-on editions and translate them in different languages. We will see, stranger things have happened before.

**AUTHORITARIANISM & PROPAGANDA
| The Puppet Master Tools**
© Marcelo Baqueroalvarez HLC 2022.
HLCControlNumber: 22-0800015-M

Paperback ISBN: 979-8-9893753-0-1
E-Book ISBN: 979-8-9893753-1-8

This Book (all versions) ISBN numbers are owned by J. Marcelo Baqueroalvarez, and published under BeeZee Vision, LLC™ and Half Life Crisis™
www.beeezeevision.com
www.halflifecrisis.com

The Printed Book and E-Book mass production, print on demand, and world-wide availability for
"**AUTHORITARIANISM AND PROPAGANDA
| The Puppet Master Tools**"
was conducted via *The Ewings Publisher, LLC.*
www.theewingspublishing.com

COVER DESIGN RIGHTS & CONCEPT

© Alicia, Marcelo, and Samantha Baqueroalvarez | HLC 2023.

The original book cover design for "**AUTHORITARIANISM & PROPAGANDA | The Puppet Master Tools**" is a collaborative effort between Alicia D. Baqueroalvarez, J. Marcelo Baqueroalvarez, and Samantha B. Baqueroalvarez.

The design depicts the mischievousness of a puppet master's deception represented by the cat who is toying with two graphic design puppets. Both puppets have SMPTE TV color bars for faces representing the absorption of projected media rhetoric.

They also lack feet because they cannot escape the constraints of their environment. One puppet has broken free from the ties of the puppet master with his right hand, symbolizing that by reading this book you will become aware of the reality hidden in plain sight.

The tumbleweeds behind represent death left by authoritarians around the world, and the erosion of truthfulness, as well as the exploited biases that separates us from one another without realizing that we are more similar that different; leaving only dried-up remains of an otherwise thriving civilization.

The world at their feet stands for the fact that this is a world- wide phenomenon, and it has been going on for as long as humans have been roaming the Earth. Also, that we are all in this together, because we all share the same planet.

The cat is emerging from a dark background to represent the fact that hidden threats are lurking in willful ignorance. The bright eyes in the cat represent the fact that somebody with bad intentions is always paying attention.

The characters' illustrations were inspired and hand-drawn using mixed media over sketch paper by Alicia D. Baqueroalvarez. The "world" was made in mixed media and paper mâché by Samantha B. Baqueroalvarez – Incorporating this piece in the artwork also stands for the new generation. The final cover design, and typographical graphic design finished piece was adapted by J. Marcelo "BeeZee" Baqueroalvarez for this book's cover.

WARNING: Reproduction in whole or in part of this book or its derivatives is strictly prohibited. Any total or partial reproduction of this book or its derivatives in any media requires the <u>written and notarized</u> authorization of the original author. That is J. Marcelo Baqueroalvarez.

Please refer to Copyright Page for Details

For official copies and written permission regarding this book, its derivatives and other original pieces from this author please contact the author via his official website as listed below:

www.halflifecrisis.com

WWW.HALFLIFECRISIS.COM

Because life is what we make of it...

www.ingramcontent.com/pod-product-compliance
Lightning Source LLC
LaVergne TN
LVHW021958060526
838201LV00048B/1609